Facets of Good Governance

Edited by
S.K. Chaturvedi
Professor & Head

Sanjeev Sharma
Reader

Originals
(an imprint of Low Price Publications)
Delhi

Distributed by
D.K. Publishers Distributors (P) Ltd.
4834/24, Ansari Road, Darya Ganj,
New Delhi-110002
Phones: 51562573, 51562575, 51562578
e-mail: dkpd@del3.vsnl.net.in
visit us at: www.dkpd.com

First Published 2005

ISBN 81-88629-45-6

Published by
Originals
(an imprint of Low Price Publications)
A-6, Nimri Commercial Centre,
Near Ashok Vihar Phase-IV, Delhi-110052
Phones: 27302453
e-mail: lpp@nde.vsnl.net.in
visit us at: www.lppindia.com

Printed at
D K Fine Art Press P Ltd.
Delhi-110052

PRINTED IN INDIA

Contributors

M.M. Sankhdhar	Formerly Professor of Political Science, University of Delhi, Delhi.
S.K. Jha	Formerly Professor and Head, Department of Political Science, Deen Dayal Upadhayaya Gorakhpur University, Gorakhpur.
S. N. Mishra	Professor of Rural Administration, Indian Institute of Public Administration, New Delhi.
R. K. Wishwakarma	Formerly Professor of Economics and Economic Administration, Indian Institute of Public Administration, New Delhi.
Jaya Tilak Guha Roy	Professor of Criminal Justice Administration, Indian Institute of Public Administration, New Delhi.
S. N. Singh	Professor Emeritus and Formerly Professor of Public Administration, Lucknow University, Lucknow.
Madhurendra Kumar	Reader, Political Science UGC Research Awardee, presently associated to Department of Political Science, CCS University, Meerut.
D. P. Chaturvedi	Reader, K. N. Government (P. G.) College, Gyanpur, Bhadohi. (U.P.).
Rekha Saraswat	Reader, Dept. of Political Science, R. G (P. G.) College, Meerut.
Brij Bhusan	Chief Executive Director, All India Institute of Management Studies and Research, Meerut.
S. K. Chaturvedi	Professor and Head, Department of Political Science, Chaudhary Charan Singh University, Meerut, Vice-President, Indian Political Science Association.

Sanjeev K. Sharma	Reader, Department of Political Science, Chaudhary Charan Singh University, Meerut, Editor, Indian Journal of Political Science.
Chaitali Pal	Research Associate, Institute of Applied Man Power Research, New Delhi.

Preface

Right from the inception of the human society peace, security, justice and development have remained ultimate objectives of the human life. In an attempt to attain these goals, it submitted itself to the coercive institutions. The philosophers from oriental and occidental world have portrayed state as an institution striving for attaining the objective of people's welfare. The famous dictum that the state is for the good of the people and continuing for ensuring a better life to them subscribes this view. Kautilyas concept of 'Rajdharma' and emperor Ashoka's concept of "Yogakshema" further support this feeling which though traversed through the medieval and modern ages got impeded by the sovereigns of the day. However, common man's struggle for good governance continued.

In India throughout the tortuous path of freedom struggle, demand for self government and good government remained one of the main agenda of debate between the colonial masters and freedom fighters. After attainment of independence founding fathers of our constitution made the state accountable to the people and ensured the individual liberty, equality and justice within the framework of a democratic, and secular republic. They directed the state to ensure welfare of one and all in the society. Attempts were made to revitalize public administration at various levels through statutory and non statutory bodies. However, despite all these efforts, the state has seemingly failed in making an impact on people's life and psyche as is evident in almost all spheres of the polity. Many unhealthy developments are being witnessed in our political and administrative setup, which deeply affect other segments of the society. It is in this context that the issue of Good Governance has become of much significance. It is at this stage that one should think whether our political regime, the process by which authority is being exercised in the management of country's economic and social life and capacity of government to design, formulate and implement public policies is responding to the people's aspirations of development in right earnest way? In this context whether we can learn something from our glorious past? Needless to mention that state-society relation in the fast changing national and global environment is required to be debated. New patterns of interaction between government and society can be observed in areas such as social welfare, environmental protection, human rights, educational and physical planning which the government of the day need to frame and perform accordingly with excellence.

'Good Governance' is a two-way traffic. If the government is committed to the people for their greatest good, the people themselves can only realize it by having a stake in the government for the sake of future and future is the place where all of us will live the rest of our lives. It is in this context that some eminent scholars have put their views to trace the fiber of good governance from unknown past to searching present. The views have been expressed by these scholars in a national seminar organized by the Department of Political Science, Chaudhary Charan Singh University, Meerut some time ago. Later, it was decided to present them in a volume for which the University Grants Commission, New Delhi, provided basic pecuniary input. Out of umpteen papers only thirteen have been culled in this volume.

At the very out set Sanjeev Kumar Sharma in his paper tries to underline the functions, duties, role and characteristics of a good, popular and dutiful king as inscribed in the Shanti Parv of the epic Mahabharata. It may be worthwhile to mention that the ancient scripture lays down a parameter while testing goodness of the governance and state.

विक्रोशन्त्यो यस्य राष्ट्रा दिध्रियन्ते दस्युमिः प्रजाः
स्पययतः मृतः सनतुजीवति, अपस्तम्ब सूत्र

The subsequent paper of Rekha Saraswat provides a vivid picture of the attempts made by the people from Neolithic age to the present age of democratization for attaining the goal of good governance and feels that governance has seldom remained good to the common man. However, a true democracy can turn the dream of the masses to a reality.

Though the aspirations of a governance which may prove good to the masses has always stirred the minds of elite and common man alike but it is seriously being debated by the scholars, administrators and political leadership now, the paper Good Governance an Overview presents understanding of the concept. In this continuation, various factors for the evaluation of good governance have been put forward by Professor S.N. Singh in his contribution to the volume. Prof. S.K. Jha advocates that there seem to be a need to review the constitution so as to improve the quality of politics and public life and inculcate a sense of moral responsibility among the people in general and those in power in particular in an attempt to achieve the goal of good governance. The same concern has been shown by the author in the subsequent paper. He feels that for removing barriers coming in the way of rule of law, an essential for effective governance, universal civil code is desired so as the twin objectives of social justice and secular polity may be attained. Dr. Madhurendra Kumar briefly surveys the concept of good governance in historical perspective, its features and underlines the hurdles being faced by it and makes a fervent appeal for finding out a strategy for sustainable human development.

Prof. S.N. Mishra and Chaitai Pal consider an ideology based political party and politicians committed to values as precursor for goodness of the governance. Needless to mention that only ideology based political parties and leadership committed to the values can keep the parliamentary democracy on right track. At the same time there is need for making the bureaucratic system pro-active, accountable and efficient is the essence of the article of Dr. D.P. Chaturvedi. Obviously it is the bureaucracy, which keep the distribution channels operative and ensure that the aspirations of the last man in the society are fulfilled. Prof. Jaya Tilak Guha Roy considers that awareness about one's own rights has enhanced the expectations of the people in a democratic system. Any laxity on the part of the system may push the society in a hostile and turbulent situation. Hence, the need of the hour is collaboration rather than confrontation between the state and civil society organizations, between government and non-government sectors. Such a cooperation may usher into an era of good governance.

Corporate sector has number of inbuilt problems in connection with the state and administrative system. Brij Bhusan has summarily placed the gamut of the corporate sector, its problems and suggestions to combat with the same. He concludes that corporate governance built upon trust, transparency and accountability can be regarded as good and effective.

The test of good governance is to create an enabling environment for the people, to enjoy long, healthy and creative lives for which the government of the day needs to take wide ranging measures for most of which is the question of ensuring security to each individual. The government of the day need to take necessary steps in the direction suggests Prof. R.K. Wishwakarma.

Late Prof. M.M. Sankhdhar has suggested on alternative frame work of governance towards attaining the goal of 'good governance' and to him 'Swedeshi' is that alternative model which may help in realizing the objectives.

Succinctly the contributors have dealt with the conceptual frame of subject matter, its evolution, significance and need to the present day society for which they suggest a wide ranging structural reforms to be brought out in the political institutions and processes so as to enhance their capabilities in fulfilling the aspirations of the masses while keeping itself committed to socio-political values with a high degree of transparency and accountability. For the purpose even the review of the constitution has been suggested by the scholars. Of late, the government constituted some committees for making suggestions in respect of attainment of the goal of good governance.

This volume may not have seen the light of the day if the contributors have not conceded to our request. We are taking this opportunity to thank them all. We pay our sincere gratitude to the Hon'ble Vice Chancellor Dr. R. P. Singh who always generously extended a helping hand in making the academic events successful and vibrant. Our colleagues on the university campus and students also deserve thanks for their unflinching support and cooperation. We also place on records all good words to the University Grants Commission for extending us financial assistance for organizing the seminar.

(S.K. CHATURVEDI)

(S.K. SHARMA)

Contents

Preface v

1. Good Governance in Ancient India
Sanjeev Kumar Sharma 1
2. Good Governance: A Historical Perspective
Rekha Sarawat 11
3. Good Governance: An Overview
S. K. Chaturvedi 29
4. Socio-Political Aspects of Good Governance
S. N. Singh 35
5. Good Governance: The Question of Reviewing the Constitution
S. K. Jha 41
6. Uniform Civil Code: A Prelude to Good Governance
S. K. Chaturvedi 61
7. Discourse on Good Governance: Some Reflections on Indian Experience
Madhurendra Kumar 69
8. Ideology free Political Parties and Value Less Politicians: A Dangerous Trend for Good Governance
S.N. Mishra and *Chaitali Pal* 79
9. Politician-Bureaucrate Relationship: A Good Governance Perspective / *D. P. Chaturvedi* 91
10. Good Governance and Human Rights: The Indian Perspective
Jaya Tilak Guha Roy 95
11. Humanizing Development—An Essence of Good Governance: A Peep in Human Development Reports
R. K. Wishwakarma 99

12. Good Governance: A Corporate Perspective
Brij Bhusan 111
13. Alternate Framework of Governance
M. M. Sankhdhar 117
Appendices 121
Select Bibliography 167
Articles 173

List of Tables

Table 1: Human Development Index 105
Table 2: Gender-related Development Index 106
Table 3: Gender Empowerment Measure 107
Table 4: Human Poverty in Developing Countries Measure 108

1

Good Governance in Ancient India

Some Notes on Kingship in *Shantiparavam* of Mahabharat

Sanjeev Kumar Sharma

Rajadharama, Dandaniti, Arthashastra, Rajyashastra and *Nitishastra* are some of the terms describing the study of politics in ancient India. *Dandaniti* is most frequently used among them. Mahabharat is presumably the first Indian treatise on the science of governance. There is one huge *Rajdharama* section discussing various aspects of governance besides *Sabhaparvam* and *Vanaparvam.* The *Rajadharma* section constitutes part of *Shantiparvam.* After the great Mahabharat war, the wining group of Pandavas headed by the eldest of them, Yudhishthira, approaches their grandfather Bhishma for guidance in running the administration of the state. Bhishma was lying on the *shar shayya* (the bed of arrows) in the war field and waiting for his death which he was said to be embracing only in Uttarayana. Yudhishthira requests Bhishma to direct him the ways of good governance. The whole episode is embodied in the *Shantiparvam* of Mahabharat. Though the discussion about the *Rajadharma* is lengthy enough and spreads into one hundred thirty chapters on *Rajadharma* and forty-two chapters on *Apaddharma,* the main theme of this voluminous part of Mahabharat is the function, duties, role and characteristics of a good, popular and dutiful king.

We know that the Mahabharat is the largest epic and constitutes eighteen parvas (sections). The key ingredient of this treatise is the description of the socio-political conditions of that period leading to the great War. But because of the very nature of Indian writings, the book essentially includes so many aspects of human life inasmuch as it has been said that it incorporates all that had happened on earth till that time. To make it worth reading, there are number of long and short stories embedded with the philosophical and enumerative body text in such a manner that one can easily get confounded with the variety of issues the book has touched upon.

It is unfortunate to note that Mahabharat as well as the most of the other early Indian writings including the Vedas, Ramayana, etc. have generally been looked upon as either literary or religious works of early Hindu society. And therefore, serious attempts to look into these grand old treatises for tracing the links of modern issues have largely been ridiculed as parochial, fundamental or otherwise. Some noteworthy works have, nonetheless, been able to put forward the basic ideas of ancient Indian society before the academic World. Eventually, even most of these works are the academic exercises by Western writers with an intention to peep into the socio-political life styles of early Indians and are based on an alien viewpoint. This shortcoming can mainly be attributed to the fact that they were simply unaware of the socio-cultural complexities of Indian society in general. Again, one of the main shortfalls of these works is to trying to locate the present days concepts and institutions in their raw form and shape in the early Indian society. This is applicable to the most of Indian writings also. But it must be safely suggested that the huge time gap between these comparisons often leads us to misunderstanding of the myths, beliefs, value-patterns, role models and functional dimensions of those societies in the light of modern yardsticks being applied for. The legacy of colonial rule, acceptance of modern democratic system, growing problems of national integration, the compulsions of multi-religious and multi-cultural secular set up, increasing allurement of westernized models of life, decline of vernacular languages and the rise of English based academia, etc. are some of the main reasons behind our general apathy towards our cultural past. To our instant dismay contemporary pressures of real politick have produced a substantial section of Indian intelligentsia which has, under the impressions of academic hegemony of the English speaking and writing West, inculcated in themselves sense of sheer disregard, indifference, disbelief, apathy, hostility and criticism for anything that can be associated with ancient India.

The scenario is comfortable for those who find it hard to go through ancient Indian writings because they are written in Sanskrit, a language that has a very strict scientific grammar and has less elasticity as compared to English. In addition to that the adoption of the model of industrialization by Pandit Jawahar Lal Nehru, the first Prime Minister of India, as the only way of the upliftment of Indian society and the adoption of globalization-liberalization model of development by Rajiv Gandhi in 1990s, the then Prime Minister of India and eventually the grandson of JL Nehru, and of course, by the succeeding governments have also led Indian academia to believe that any endeavour to look into our ancient past is purely futile. Leaving apart the political aspects of this attitude of Indian academia, the greatest loss incurred to because of this has been in the field of serious research studies in social sciences. Though it cannot be argued that the ancient Indian writings possess emphatic solutions to all the present day conflicts, yet it can be stated forthwith that serious studies of ancient Indian literature with social science view point would definitely pave the way of better understanding of the Indian mindset and thereby prove immensely helpful in shaping our socio-political values and institutions in an indigenous manner. It is in this backdrop that the present paper tries to find, locate, understand and narrate some aspect of good governance discussed at length in the *Shantiparvam* of Mahabharat with special reference to kingship.

There is one very interesting anecdote in chapter twenty third of *Shantiparvam* in Mahabharat. After the Great War, Yudhisthir finds that he is the king of a state, which is carved upon the dead bodies of millions of warriors, his relatives and great people of that period and thus leaving behind thousands of widows and orphans. The aftermath of the bloodshed of war creates a sense of alienation in the mind of Yudhisthir. He expresses his wish to renunciate the kingship and goes to the forest for *tapasya*. Bhima, Arjun, Draupadi, etc. go on persuading Yudhisthir to forget about the results of war and get into action as a dutiful king to fulfil the responsibilities towards the population.[1] Finally, Vyas, the grand old man of the family narrates a story of two brothers, which serves the purposes of suggesting the proper functional role to Yudhisthir as well as putting forward the functional differentiation of the various organs of state.

The story begins with two brothers—Shankha and Likhit, having two separate ashrams. Both of the brothers were involved in hard worship and *tapasya*. Once, Likhit visited the ashram of Shankha and saw a number of trees loaded with ripe fruits. Keeping in mind the ownership of the ashram in his brother, Likhit started eating fruits. When he was enjoying these fruits, his brother Shankha came and asked him. "Where did you get these fruits from?" Likhit answered. "These are from your ashram, my brother" "But you have not sought my permission to eat these fruits and thus you have committed theft," said Shankha, "What should I do now?" asked Likhit. Shankha suggested, "You are guilty of theft. The duty and authority to punish the thieves rests in the king. You must approach the king, tell him the truth and ask him for deciding your punishment." Likhit obeyed his brother and went to king Sudyumna, and narrated the whole story. Primarily, the king observes that when Likhit has already made a confession about this theft, and him being a hermit, there was no need for any further punishment. Repentance is more than a punishment. But Likhit insists upon performing the role of king and the king, finally orders Likhit's hands to be cut. Likhit, after receiving the punishment at the hands of the king, returns to his brother and requests him to forgive his deeds. Shankha says that he had nothing against him. Likhit had violated the rules of *Dharma* and the king only could decide the fine for the crime committed by him. Now when you has received the fine, I through my spiritual power provide you new hands. The moral of the story is that everybody in the society has to perform some specified roles, and any violation of the rules against the norms of the society and therefore, requires punishment from the authority designated for that the purpose.[2]

Shantiparvam of Mahabharat provides a great deal of information about political ideas of ancient India and is indisputably the finest treatise on ancient Indian polities. Some of the writers have observed that the sovereignty was embodied in the kind in ancient India Thus royal sovereignty was the true symbol of the authority of the state.[3] The king, according to Vyas, should protect warriors, elite and intellectuals.[4] He should involve people with excellence in *Anvikshiki, Tryai, Varta, Dandaniti* in most of the functions of the state.[5]

According to Mahabharat the sphere of the state activity is extended to almost all the walks of life. The state in ancient India was, thus, the main centre of the society and the primary equipment of the welfare of the people. It was in this backdrop that a serious, methodical and proper study and prescription of the functions and various aspects of state was considered necessary. The king is the first and foremost part of the state. Most of the well being of the state depends on the king. Therefore, all the writers of ancient Indian polity had given the king prime importance.

Basham observes that 'though India had no formal political philosophy, the science of statecraft was much cultivated, and a number of important text books on this topic have survived. *Dandaniti*, the administration of force or *Rajniti*, the conduct of kings, was a severely practical science, and the texts cursorily dismiss the more philosophical aspect of politics, but give comparatively detailed advice on the organization of thc state and the conduct of governmental affairs.'[6]

It is the duty of the king to seek and promote the welfare of its subject.[7] The king must be compassionate to the people of all section of society and concentrate on the welfare of the people.[8] The best king possesses following qualities: intellect, renunciation, awareness of the weaknesses of the enemies, good looks, capacity to be fair and just to all the sub-sections, quickness in decision, softness in behaviour, industrious, hardworking, forsightedness, indifference to self-pride and control over anger.[9] Kingship in ancient India may be termed as 'benevolent, paternalistic autocracy bound down by many instructions of service to the people.' King was considered to be a servant of the people. His main functions were protection, prosperity, maintenance of righteousness and

Dharma and doing impartial justice. He was not expected to act according to his personal likes or dislikes but only according to the wishes and will of the people. He was expected to devote his life to the service and the welfare of the subjects of his state. Mahabharat expects the king to deploy secret and trusted agents to ascertain the views of his subjects about his conduct, actions, and reputation. Mahabharat essentially believes that tyrannical tendencies of the king can best be curbed by moral, spiritual and religious sanctions. Therefore, at one place it has been observed that the king decided the course of life of his subjects while the course of life of the king has to be decided by the priests. This depicts the control of the forces of knowledge and reason over the forces of physical power. Any dereliction of duty would have invited so many punishments for the king during and after his life that following the path of *Dharma* is the only way for their existence. *Dharma*, it was said, upholds all the creatures. The king was to perform his duties according to *Dharma* otherwise he would invite entry into the hell and this notion supposedly served as a great deterrent. The story of the origin of the king emphasizes that king has come into existence for the maintenance of peace and *Dharma* on the earth. Mahabharat preaches of the paternalism of the king.

While requesting Bhishma to suggest him the ways of good governance, Yudhishthir himself says that *Rajadharma* is all comprehensive. It is inclusive of *Dharma, Artha* and *Kama* (*Trivarga*).[10] *Rajadharma* only is able to control the world and keep the people under the restraint of *maryada*.[11] It prevents the people from committing sins and wrongs.[12] Bhishma says that one should first acquire the king than only wife and wealth because unless there is no king to protect him, there will be no security either for wife or for wealth.[13] Bhishma enumerates Brihaspathi, Vishalakhsa, Shukra, Indra, Manu, Bharadwaj and Gaurshira as main propounders of *Rajadharma* before him.[14]

Brihaspathi says that whatever *Dharma* is there on the earth, that is all because of the king. It is his presence, which prevents the people from killing each other.[15] The property, sons, daughters, women, vehicle, jewelry, clothings, houses, wealth, etc. all get secure from any loot or robbery only when there is a king performing his duties of providing good condition of living and security, proper administration welfare policies and decision-making. He has to make necessary arrangements so that people may not deviate from the path of *Dharma*, agriculture is flourished, business gets a boost, social rituals get performed, moral bindings are adhered to, students indulge in studies and hermits in *tapasya*, justice prevails, fearlessness proliferates, violence diminishes and all is well in the state.[16] The king should employ efficient intelligent and visionary people for ascertaining the truth while doing justice because the state can remain intact only on true justice.[17]

The king should assume different roles according the different situations as according to the needs of the hour, such as destroying the enemies, inflicting punishments upon the wicked, bestowing rewards upon the good, fining offenders, etc. The first and foremost duty of the king was to protect the life and property of the people from all kinds of invasions and creation of an environment of righteousness in his state. A king incapable of protecting the people is useless. The restraint of *Dharma* can only facilitate the conditions for the prevalence of righteousness and the promotion of the material well-being of the people, which is the essential duty of the king. The king should be wise and courageous, only then he can make the earth habitable and comfortable for the people.

The king's main function, as observed by Ray, was to maintain the established social order. Since a society was believed to remain well ordered only so long as each individual observed his personal and caste *Dharma*, the king's *Dharma* consisted in maintaining the rule of *Dharma* is society at large. In concrete terms, this meant that he was to facilitate the study of *Vedas* and philosophy, encourage the development of industry and commerce, maintain proper relations between different castes, ensure the observance of parental, filial, matrimonial and other duties, enforce *Dharma* pertaining to different stages of individual life, and so on. The king derived his authority from the fact that he needed it to maintain *Dharma*.[18]

The king should employ persons of intellect and renunciatory approach into the main walks of state. King should of collect revenue from the l/6th of the income of the people, by imposing suitable taxes, by instituting financial punishment to the defaulters and criminals and getting some amount as remuneration or reward for protecting traders.[19] By collecting taxes from the populace as the instruction of *Dharma*, the king is directed to govern the state with the welfare of subjects in his mind.[20] The king should remain involved in the well-being of his public and be prepared for anything possible for their protection. All duties of the king should be performed according to the provisions of *Dharma* which are to be respected in every eventuality, not by the king but also by his public. The goods done by the public through adherence to the principles of *Dharma*, would add its one fourth into the goods performed by king himself.[21] Bhisma prescribes five assistants of the king. Interestingly one of the most important assistants among the five is one who acts according to the *Dharma*, is not biased. He behaves impartially, does not divulge information and never involves himself into wrongs This emphatically makes clear that the suggestions to the king must emanate from such people which the king can have faith in.[22] The secret information of the state should be shared with such people who are dear to the king, who are knowledgeable and who have extraordinary control over their faculties.[23] The king should involve all the populace in their respective duties and instruct them to perform their assigned functions according to *Dharma*.[24] Even when the king does not possess any of the specified qualities, only by protecting his people from any physical, moral and economic aggression, the king fulfils his duties well.[25]

Seven parts of the state according to Mahabharat are King, Mantri, Kosha, Danda, Mitra, Rashtra, Nagar.[26] King should employ spies at various places for ascertaining the activities of the enemies. He should also depute spies so as to ascertain the trends of the won people at various public places.[27]

The main sources of income of the king are described as a sixth part, fair calculation of the yield, fines and forfeitures upon offenders, traders and merchants in return of the protection guaranteed to them. The taxes should never be imposed unreasonably. Therefore, the overall happiness of the subjects, strict adherence to truth and *Dharma* and true sincere behaviour are main duties of the king.

If the king commits wrongs and sins *Dandaniti* may get destroyed and *Rajadharma* humiliated resulting in the absence of the sense of right and wrong among the people.[28] The king is the lord of the people, if he performs his duties of deputing his populate into their respective *Dharma* and protecting them properly, even the gods do not defy him.[29] At the same time, Mahabharat strongly condemns anarchy. It prescribes for the people of kingless state to welcome any invading king because the anarchy is the most grave sin on earth.[30] Anarchic state has no security for its citizens, property, wealth, women, servants, poor and weak.[31]

Rajdharma of the king includes fighting war for the protection of the population, being compassionate for the living creatures, knowing the public behaviour, providing security to the people, eliminating the problems of the subjects and reducing the plight of the masses.[32] The king by providing better conditions of life, facilitates generation of fearless society.[33] The Mahabharat explicitly sanctions revolt against a king who is oppressive or fails in his function of protection, saying that such a ruler is no king at all, and should be killed like a mad dog.[34]

The king must be cautions and careful in appointing his counsels. Their qualities as well as function and duties have also been discussed in detail in various chapters of *Shantiparvam*. The king has been directed to appoint people of caliber, integrity, reason, compassion, restraint, efficient, reliable, just, and knowledge as his counsels. And these should be assigned duties according to their skill and intentions.[35] The king must be vigilant enough to protect his *Kosha* because if the *Kosha* is insecure the king is doomed to vanish.[36] The secret informations of the state should never be divulged to those who are idiots, liars, suspicious, and greedy people.[37] The cabinet of the king should contain four Brahmins with knowledge of Vedas, eight Kshatriyas with immense physical force and power, twenty-one Vaishs with prosperity, three Sudras with benevolence and good manners and one Suta knowing *Puranas*.[38] The decisions of this cabinet must be disseminated throughout the state so as to apprise all the citizens about the decisions of the sate and invite their suggestions and critical remedial measures.[39] The king should punish the offenders in consonance with the intensity of their offences. If the offender is rich, he must be deprived of his wealth and if he is poor, he must be sent to jail.[40] The qualities of the messenger, gatekeeper, bodyguard and the chief of the army have also been given in detail in this section of Mahabharat.

Again, a few chapters discuss the administration and law and order of the capital city,[41] revenue collection,[42] taxation,[43] military functioning[44] and the Republics.[45] These discussions prove the existence of well planned and consistent thought process about state in ancient India The king has to perform all his duties according to *Dharma*, he is forbidden to do such things, which the people with reason have denied, and he should protect the people as well as *Dharma*.[46] The functionaries of the state should be assigned roles according to their ability and skill. This rule must never be violated because this may lead to inefficiency causing in anguish amongst the subject.[47] The power and authority of the king is designated in him by the Almighty God himself and the king has come into existence only for the protection of the people.[48] The people and king are complementary to each other. Therefore, in case of any emergency they must protect each other.[49] Where the public and the visitors to the state are unhappy and curious about their living, there the king is condemnable.[50] The king has to carry the load of running the state properly such as the cow's carry the bullockcart.[51]

A king without force and power is worthless because he will loose the *Kosha*, and if there is no Kosha, there will be no army, and where there is no army, there can be no state.[52] Therefore, the king must regulate such norms for the people in his state which are not only binding upon them but also making them happy about the affairs of the state.[53] Mahabharat discusses the phenomenon of power at length and concludes that power is more important than *Dharma* in relation to *Rajadharma* because with power only, *Dharma* can be established.[54] The relationship of even the friends and foes and determined according to power.[55]

From the above sketch of the characteristics, roles, duties, functions and qualities of the king described and discussed in *Shantiparvam* of

Mahabharat at length, we may very safely conclude that the main duties of the king were maintenance of *Varnashram* system, protection of the people, establishment of rules and general principles of activity in the state, appointment of royal servants, inspection of the functionaries, economic well being and social welfare of the people of the state. Besides, day to day functions of the king have also been discussed and analyzed in detail in this part of Mahabharat. We have to look into some other aspects also for understanding the administrative, financial and participatory dimensions of ancient Indian polity. This paper is a modest attempt in this direction and undertakes to peep into further details of structural and functional aspects of ancient Indian politics. Some of the traits of the kings described and enumerated in this treatise may very well pave the way of political socialization of our newly recruited political leadership.

References

1. This discussion is spread into thirty-six chapters of *Shantiparvam*.
2. *Mahabharat*, Vth Part, Shantiparvam, Geeta Press, Gorakhpur, rep. 2001. (23.44).
3. See, H.N Sinha, *Sovereignty Ancient Indian Polity*, London, Luzac & Co., 1938, pp. 18-19, UN Ghoshal, *A History of Hindu Political Theories*, Oxford University Press, London, 1923, p. 84.
4. Mahabharat, *op.cit.*, (24.17).
5. *Ibid.*, (24.18).
6. A.L. Basham, *The Wonder That Was India*, Rupa, & Co., New Delhi, 1967 reprint 1995, p.80.
7. Mahabharat, *op.cit.*, ((3.1.2)
8 *Ibid.*, (55.36)
9. *Ibid.*, (57.30-32)
10. *Ibid.*, (55.31.4)
11. *Ibid.*,(65.5)
12. *Ibid.*, (55.7)
13. *Ibid.*, (57.41)
14. *Ibid.*, (58.1-4)
15. *Ibid.*, (68.8)
16. *Ibid.*, (68.14-36)
17. *Ibid.*, (69.28)
18. B.N. Ray, *Tradition and Innovation in Indian Political Thought*, Ajanta, Delhi, 1998, p. 13.

19. Mahabharat, *op.cit.*, (71.10).
20. *Ibid.*, (71.11).
21. *Ibid.*, (75.6-8).
22. *Ibid.*, (80.3-5).
23. *Ibid.*, (81.3).
24. *Ibid.*, (60.19).
25. *Ibid.*, (60.20).
26. *Ibid.*, (69.64-65).
27. *Ibid.*, (69.52).
28. *Ibid.*, (65.24).
29. *Ibid* , (65 29).
30. *Ibid.*, (67.6-7).
31. *Ibid.*, (67.12-16).
32. *Ibid.*, (64.27).
33. *Ibid.*, (64.28).
34. A.L. Basham, *op.cit.*, pp. 88-89.
35. Mahabharat, *op.cit.*, (80.25).
36. *Ibid.*, (82.4).
37. *Ibid.*, (83.37).
38. *Ibid.*, (85.7-11).
39. *Ibid.*, (85.12).
40. *Ibid.*, (85.20).
41. *Ibid.*, (86).
42. *Ibid.*, (87).
43. *Ibid.*, (88).
44. *Ibid.*, (100).
45. *Ibid.*, (107).
46. *Ibid.*, (89.3-5,93.22, 94.10).
47. *Ibid.*, (119.4.6-7).
48. *Ibid.*, (12 1.39-42).
49. *Ibid.*, (130.30).
50. *Ibid.*, (130.34).
51. *Ibid.*, (132.14).
52. *Ibid.*, (133.4).
53. *Ibid.*, (133.13).
54. *Ibid.*, (134.6).
55. *Ibid.*, (138.139).

2

Good Governance: A Historical Perspective

Rekha Saraswat

This paper is an effort in critically studying the concept of good governance. It carries a sequential study of good governance, right form its etymological form to its epistemological development. Its expectations are put to test in different scales and levels of growth. Its reality is discussed with an ontological perspective in mind. Its prospects are highlighted with various value judgments. Overall, this paper tries to make a non-biased factual interpretation and analysis and a non-hypocritical future anticipation of good governance. The perspective is worldwide, the comparison is all round but the persuasions are ethnic. The study-span is right from the period of to the Modern-Man of the 20th century. The political institutions and the art of administration of this path of progress have been traced to arrive at certain conclusions about their all round development process.

The history of human progress began with the Eolithic Man. He is said to have gone beyond barbarism the moment he made a pounding tool. Both historians and social scientists accepted this as his cultural advancement. No wonder, even now, pounding is taken as the measure of a man's progress The harder he is able to pound, the more successful he is taken in life. Perhaps this is what Hobbes meant by his force theory!

Next came the Paleolithic man. He wandered and hunted with stone-hatchets but came back in the nights to sleep in his cave. He wore animal skin around his waist and is now called The old-stone-age-man. But he made law of governance. He created religion, wrote stories, imagined and the concept of games on the hand and developed the value of justice and social order on the other. This shows that wherever and whenever there was order, creativity grew as a natural by-product. This statement was proved in the later stages too.

The third in the line of pre-historic man was the Neolithic-man. He is also known as the new stone -age-man now. Still stone aged, because even now he was making tools and arms with stone. He made handled axe with hewn stone and knives with bone and flint. Yet, the Neolithic-age man invented the famous bows and arrows of Ramayana and Mahabharat. It was for the first time, in this age, that man began to use wood. He made huge houses out of wood and its bark, constructed villages on lakes by building them on long wooden platforms, which floated on the lakes as bridges. This was a huge leap forward for humanity because from this time onward man learned to settle at one place. He started to sow seeds and grow crops. He became an agriculturist. It was from here that political institutionalization began to take shape. It was, again, from here that man began to realize the importance of living together, in-groups. He formed small tribes, each one controlled by a chieftain. Some chieftains, who lived nearby, formed leagues to remain united against unexpected dangers and calamities. (One can't help but marvel at their strong common sense at such an early stage of their development). The Iroquois confederations of the Neolithic prove this point. They lived in clans of maternal families. Four or more clans formed Phratries. Two Phratries formed a Tribe. A chieftain ruled each tribe. Many chieftains together formed a Council. And they worked in a League. These chieftains were appointed on merit alone, and were most unceremoniously recalled if they didn't deliver the goods to their tribes. Thus, it can be concluded without any doubt, that the concept of federal governments was initiated, as early as 7000 years before Christ was born, by the Neolithics. A system which is even now considered as the most modern form of governance! Here, it proves that any rationally arrived at decision and logically derived truth holds true forever. And this is the main reason why nothing of great consequence was added to man's progress, right from the age of the Neolithics, up till the age of the Industrial revolution of the 18th century.

Next, in the group of early types of man, came the metal-age-man. First, there were stones, then wood and now it was the use of metals– copper, bronze, iron etc. that brought changes in the life of man. His tools and weapons became more sophisticated, strong and durable. As a natural corollary, his social and political relationships also became more complex, competitive and stable. He institutionalized religion, society as well as politics. He became interested in wars, in conquests, in accumulating property. This ominous trend has not stopped even now. He used religion, social -norms as well as political institutions to fulfill these newfound interests. Even now this farce is continuing. Patriarchal leaders headed his political institution on a simple logic that " fight the war for us and become our natural leader". The father of the family was the first political administrator. He led in wars, owned family-property and gave judgment upon local disputes. He used temples, religion and the concept of God to cement people together. People began to obey his commands out of necessity. During peace times such leaders were respected and followed because people knew that these leaders were ready to sacrifice their lives for them when need would arise.

Here we have to remember that the earlier tribal leaders, family heads or army chieftains could govern because they could really serve their people and help them lead a peaceful, just and better life. It also shows that the governments were truly representative in their nature even in that primitive society. And whatever their form might have been; divine, of-force or contractual, the leaders were recalled from power if they did not serve the people to their satisfaction. And this was a natural process. So our pre-historic man had very logically and rationally defined the concept of good governance even when his political-institutions were not developed properly. There were two prime reasons for the organization of governments. One, maintaining the safety and security of the people. Two, providing justice to them. They used the fear of taboos and divine punishment to control anti-social elements. And thus the primitive man gradually became a law-abiding person. (Lex-Talon, *i.e,.*, eye for eye and tooth for tooth was substituted to a more refined way of implementation of punishment laws). Fine amounts, jail exile and corporal punishments were categorically determined.

The pre-literate stage carries the longest history of man, more than ten lakh years long. It paved the way for modern governance methods, and its concepts of ' confederation' and representation' are still considered the best forms of governance. We have no doubt, developed mechanically, technically and scientifically; but the nascent truth of human endeavor for happiness and its scale of measurement remains, ad-infinitum, the same.

It is due to their continuous, honest and innocent efforts that the ancient empires, which came next in the sequence, were so advanced, developed and literate. The first, in the four notable ancient empires were the Egyptian-Empire, established on the eastern part of the Fertile-Crescent. These empires can be divided into three kinds, in the sequence of their formation, to know about their governance pattern. The first were the pyramid-age-empires. They remained between 3400-2500 B.C. The kings of these empires were absolute rulers, called as the Menes and the Pharaoh Cheops who claimed to be the ' Sons of God'. The subject also believed in their divinity. They were military heads. They directed industries. They supervised public works. And they controlled all the resources. They were autocratic, accepting absolutely no interference from the masses. A huge plethora of civil servants worked for them. And they were equally bureaucratic and arrogant. The empires were, naturally, as a result, strong, centralized and vast.. They stretched right up to Palestine, Phoenicia and Syria. The people were simply docile and servile, without any individual freedom or say in the state matters. They were supposed to follow the dictates, of the kings and their bureaucrats without any doubts or objections. We should remember that the success of those empires was measured in terms of the strength of their kings and the vastness of their sizes and never in terms of the progress and development of their subjects. So, good governance had an absolutely different meaning than what it is today. But as is always the case with absolute monarchies, the Pharaoh Cheops became smug, over confident and indifferent. They got absolutely dependent upon their spoilt bureaucrats, who 'ruled the roast and with candor'. And this continued for five hundred years, giving rise to an absolute anarchy, which is always, a natural corollary of autocracy.

Confusion and chaos, therefore, became the hallmarks of the next empire (in the line of the ancient empires). It was called as the feudal-age-empire. The large centralized empires were disintegrated into small weak states, ruled by powerful, selfish priests, rival nobles and corrupt kings' officials. " The masses, as usual, mistook it for liberalism" But nothing changed for them. They were put to further sufferings, poverty and continuous warfare. They were simply used as cannon fodder in the wars and could not dream for themselves. The situation, today, in India is almost similar. If we take the history of our recent past, first there were British who built a strong empire over us. Then, after Independence, came Congress, with J.L. Nehru at the realm of affairs. Nehru was wearing the invisible peruke of an imperialistic benevolent king, whom the masses followed as if by divine command. His hold was so strong that he left a legacy of a stubborn, centralized control over the country. As a result, the bureaucracy became answerable to none. And the same chaos, the same disorder, the same corruption became the order of the day, that was seen during the pyramid-empire days. The masses suffered in the same way. It was, in no way, good governance. Then came the era of coalition government and regional governments. Caste-based, community-based, religion-based, sectoral, and state-level-local leaderships mushroomed. Their harvest is still blooming. Here too, the people took it as a symbol of liberalism, but it did not improve their plight. The citizens are as helpless and as hopeless about their future as they were before. The wheel has taken many full circles. The despotic Pharaohs, the ruthless Feudal, the autocratic empires, all of them, have always used their governments to their own benefit and moulded these according to their own convenience.

The feudal age witnessed materialistic advances, our age witnessed technological advances, but in both the cases the benefits did not seep down to the common man, to the masses.

The masses, thus, suffered for more, than three hundred years, under the feudal empires till 1580 B.C. Then came the era of new Egyptian Empires. Emperors like Thitmos-I (1545-1514 B.C.) & Thitmos II (1479-1447 B.C.), known as the Napoleons of Egypt who conquered their ways to the top. Creative and constructive rulers like Queen Hatshepsut (1501-1479 B.C.), for the first time tried to help the people to develop, but continued internal dissentions of powerful feudal nobility did not allow this to happen. They weakened the New Empires. As a result, the Persians ultimately conquered them and with this the era of Egyptian Empires came to a pitiable end. Why empires, with good governance rose and why they fell? Was it destiny? Tides rise high to fall the next moment? No. A political analyst can't seek such mystical solutions to the human problems. Many reasons if analyzed, in the present context, may be listed out. But one thing stands out clear, that in both the rise and the fall of the civilizations, the common man never rose. He only fell to greater depths, every time, when a new empire arose. He was sometimes a laborer, sometimes a slave, sometimes a constructor and sometimes a serf: simply a peg in the wheel of the empire's development. He only strengthened the empires but they gave him nothing in the bargain. Yet civilizations don't bloom on the carcasses of human despair. And this has been proved umpteen times in the history of the rise and fall of glorious empires!

Out of the various civilizations, which flourished on the eastern part of the Fertile Crescent, where people of the Tigris Euphrates Valley lived, three may be used here as paradigms for the study of standard successful governance at that time. They were the Sumerians, the Babylonians and the Assyrinas.

The Sumerians had a powerful political system, which they continued for fifteen hundred years. Their societies was wealthy, well developed and law abiding, They lived in monarchies. But their kings were messengers of God, called as Patesti (meaning tenant farmer). The king was supposed to be sent by God on lease, and this lease was to be renewed every year at the time of a festival celebrated in the honor of God. Each city had one such king who was a great man but still he did not represent God. He was a servant of God. The laws were said to be made by God. He was simply there to implement them, that too, with the help of God. His main role was to collect offerings from the people, in the name of God, as taxes are collected today, in the name of public of public welfare. Wars were usually fought for land and water. Floods would destroy these cities but the Sumerians would rebuild them, each time stronger than before. Ur, Lagesh, Umma and Nipur are some examples of the strong cities that they built. The city of Ur is still there (in parts) as a monument of their exceptional architecture, which was built in 2298 B.C. The difference between the earlier Egyptian culture and the Sumerian culture can be seen quite vividly here. Earlier the masses were living as serfs under the Pharaohs who spent their lives building temples, and pyramids, many times for as long as twenty years only to make their kings immortal, at the cost of their own lives and property. On the other hand, the Sumerian citizens built cities, dams, roads and other public utility items. They devised a script for writing which was adapted by later cultures. They made the moon calendar, and started a system of numerals. They provided the oldest center of scientific observatory. They invented the wheel and the wheeled vehicle. Jurisprudence, mathematics, graphs, natural sciences, botanical & chemical names are their contributions. All these were the achievements of the 2nd millennium B C. yet they are even now helping the humanity in the 2nd millennium A D. But look at the irony! The Egyptian civilization is still being remembered through the arts and aesthetics of its royal Pyramids, temples and historical monuments. While on the other hand the Sumerian civilization is not so much known by its name to the common man, although it gave us science, maths, the calendar and every thing that was of use to the common man. Whom should we blame for that? Should we blame the patrician bent of minds of our historians or the legal attitude of our intellectuals? The Egyptians gave us an aristocratic civilization while the Sumerians gave us a democratic culture. Whose governance should be taken as good if measured according to the present standards, is an open question for the reader to analyze and answer.

Next in the sequence of ancient empires were the Babylonians. The Babylonians reaped the harvest of the Sumerians. Hamurabi (2123-2081), the greatest king of this age, united all the prosperous cities of the Sumerians and established a centralized rule. But in sharp contrast to the Sumerian kings, he did not call himself a servant or messenger of God. He declared himself to be in direct league with ' Sun-God'. He claimed that Sun explained the laws of the kingdom to him directly and gave him the authority to implement them in his own way. He borrowed heavily from the Sumerian laws, codifying them and adding severe punishments to their sanctity. He got these laws carved upon high stone shafts for the people to follow. (One such stone is still available in that land.) The principle of Lex Talonis was prevalent there, but after due trial by the jury.

Hamurabi wielded absolute power and his subjects solely depended on his mercy. He was a patriarch and governed with an iron hand. He took full advantage of the hallow of the divine powers around him. His people borrowed the critical and analytical mind of the Sumerians. They developed measurement units of length, cubic capacity, time and weight. Astronomy, archeology, history, medicine, grammar, lexicography and philosophy were initiated. They were intellectuals in the real senses of the word. But how could people develop and prosper under the centralized governance of a monarch! And what was the difference between the Egyptian Pharaoh and the Babylonian Hamurabi! These are questions whose answers would easily set standards of good governance for the present times too!

Hamurabi was a patriarch who took his country as his family. He punished the poor and the rich with equal justice. Rather he made the rich to pay more as fine for their crimes. Women, widows and orphans were always treated with special care. Women had greater rights than men within their families, in properties, in divorce, in business and in professions. Laws were made to protect the lower classes as well as the slaves. Slaves could marry, own property and pass it on to children, even though their masters treated them as personal properties.

While Pharaohs were simply warriors and nothing else, the Babylonian kings were constructive builders, benevolent administrators and strict organizers. They left the result for us to assess. Even absolute monarchs could deliver good governance, if their subjects, the masses, were treated well and felt that justice was assured to all on an equal basis. Although the king called himself divine, but it did not make him despotic towards his subjects. He worked hard to improve the life of his subjects on this Earth. The last on the eastern part of the Fertile Crescent was the Assyrian ancient empire. It borrowed the working-culture' from the Babylonians but its political values were not the same. Its kings were ruthless aggressors and for three hundred years their mighty armies kept winning one battle after another. Sargon 2nd (722-705) and later his son Sennacherib (705-681 B.C.) conquered the whole of Fertile Crescent. They captured the entire area right up to the borderlands of Egypt. But the whole story and glory came to a gory end in 606 B.C. when Persians destroyed this Assyrian empire most relentlessly. The Assyrian governance was military governance. The king was actually a war general. His army was the main wielder of power. It had latest weaponry with it. The king controlled the whole empire through messengers and self-appointed governors. The frightened subjects could not make any noteworthy artistic or scientific inventions, creations or discoveries. The only everlasting creditable contribution by this empire was the establishment of the postal system, which was later adopted by the Persians and passed on to all coming generations of the world.

The Assyrian Empire may have been successful in conquering lands but under no stretch of imagination can it be called good governance! It only had a military relationship with its subjects! People's main purpose of living was restricted to recruitment in the king's army, to be killed in the battlefield for the egotistic fancies of their rulers!

On the western part of the Fertile Crescent, out of the Hittites, the Aramaeans the Hebrews and the Phoenicians, only the Hebrews need a mention here due to their uniqueness is governance. These imaginative people never felt the necessity of a living human king. They considered God as their king and every man in the kingdom had a direct access to him. Every man could do what he felt was right according to the dictates of his own conscience. And therefore, the northern part of their kingdom, Palestine (Israel), which had given a fertile valley to them, the people worshipped the Golden Calf. They were wealthy and materialistic in their philosophy. While on the southern part of Palestine (Judah), where God was not liberal and the land were barren and rocky, the people worshipped the poor shepherd with the calf. They were fatal in their attitude and exalted a life of misery and destitution. The Hebrews subserviated every thing to religion. Their king, in the center, was a necessary evil. He only maintained order and protected the freedom of speech. Their greatest contribution was the Old Testament, which served as the founding stone for Christianity. But politically the Hebrews were the most insecure people. Saul (1028-1013 B.C.) could unite the twelve tribes of Hebrews for the first time, but was eaten by the warrior class of Philistines. Later David (10 13-973 B.C.) and then his son Solomon (973-933 B.C.) reunited the tribes, but in 930 B.C., again, were divided due to the haughtiness of their own wealthy northern part (Israel). They were thus weak and were continuously conquered by the neighbouring kings, sometimes by the Chaldeans and sometimes by the Assyrians. They were taken as slaves to different kingdoms. Some of them fled to Egypt and came back to Jerusalem only when the Egyptians and Chaldeans defeated the Assyrians. So, their ' good governance' was left in the hands of God who ironically never came to their rescue when enemies defeated them and tortured them! This is a very crucial and sharp illustration of how good governance is messed up, if left in the hands of religion. 'Good Governance' did not give salvation to the Hebrews from the Earthy Hell. But, again the biggest contribution of the Hebrew culture was the development of the concept of individualism through a religious logic only. They believed that each human being is an extension of God's spirit and an element of his holiness is found in each person. And so no one's self-esteem should be violated or it would be a direct disrespect to God. How beautifully they taught the lesson of equality and brotherhood can be seen here! Although they used religion to justify the respectability of each individual, but their God was a benevolent ruler, who ruled through love. He was austere and stern yet used mercy almost always to give man another chance to mend his ways. No doubt, all our present elements of democracy (although scientifically rationalized now) seem to be a direct heritage of the Hebrew culture!

The Phoenicians (another ancient empire) on the western side of the Fertile Crescent organized city-states as a form of government (that was later followed by the Greeks). Many city-states together formed colonies with one city serving as the coordinating state for all of them. But it could not dominate or control any member state of the colony. Each city-state had a king who was mostly autocratic and despotic. One can conclude from this that the federal form of government that was introduced much earlier by the Neolithic-man was being used in a stricter manner here. The city-states were totally autonomous, a demand that is not accepted even now in our states. They were not agriculturists because the land between Lebanon Mountains and the Mediterranean Sea was not fertile. They were excellent traders and craftsmen. They collected exceptional items from various empires around them and traded them with the states that demanded them. They built temples for King Solomon at Jerusalem. They built furniture for the royal palaces of Assyrian kings. Their carvings on ivories and craftsmanship on gold, silver brass, wood and iron were appreciated the world over. They dyed clothes in beautiful patterns, wove them and stitched them into attractive clothing. They made combs, platters and dishes out of glass, ivory and bronze. To facilitate themselves in their trades they built their cities at strategic points along the Mediterranean. The biggest contribution of the Phoenicians was the forming of alphabets (the 22 consonants.) The Greeks later added five vowels to them and thus language was scripted. They introduced pen, ink and paper in Europe, an ever-lasting contribution to the world society. Their culture was borrowed heavily by the Greeks and passed on to the Western civilization. What was the form of government that helped the Phoenicians to contribute so much to the progress of man's creativity? Was it creativity or simply a tool of competitive trade developed out of necessity? Nowhere is the condition of the masses discussed in detail. But an inference could be drawn in reference and comparison with the earlier Assyrians kings who were equally despotic and autocratic. They used their people as killers but the Phoenician kings used their people as creators. The change was laudable. Could it be a good effect of the Hebrew culture? Could it subdue the wild instincts of these kings and make them aspire for constructive things? Or was it pure diplomacy that restrained them from fighting with their neighboring kingdoms? After all, the Phoenicians had to keep their neighbor markets open for selling their products to them. Modern concepts of International Relations were being born. Why their despotism has been subdued and not been highlighted in later political accounts and literature in a derogatory manner? This question has only one answer, and that is, their cultural contributions to the world helped them to get their bad governance pardoned in the annals of history!

Another ancient empire which needs reference here is the Aegean empire. The Aegean and the Persians are considered to be the forerunners of the later classical civilization. A special mention of the Aegean kingdom is necessary here, because of a very special kind of governance that was followed by it. A governance-system which appears so whimsical and so inhuman now!

The Aegean king was called as Minos, which meant a priest king, representing the bull God. Later he was also called as the son of Zeus. The Minos had to go through a kind of test after every nine years to prove his good governance. He had to go to the sanctuaries of God and give details to God personally about his rule of the past nine years. If God were satisfied by his report, he would allow him to go back and rule again for another nine years. How God could be contacted by the Minos, has not been mentioned! If we try to believe that the king used this gimmick to keep his subjects under control, it can be accepted as a diplomatic device to restrict unruly people. But what followed in that process was extremely contemptible. Seven young men and seven young women were sacrificed to please God for the safe return of the king from his Sanctuaries. If the king returned safe and sound (which he always did) he would rule for nine more years people were sacrificed like animals for his sake, what respect he might be giving them as subjects! What might have been their fate in the normal day to day unimaginable far cry for the Aegean!

But people don't forget and they don't forgive too. These very people who were frightened of the Godliness of their kings came out to openly support the Persians. The Persians were invaders who came to conquer their land, but Aegean people welcomed them as deliverers who would relieve them of their own kings' atrocities. The Persian king Cyrus and his son Cambyses were successful rulers, because they formed the greatest political empires of antiquity. Wherever they went as conquerors, they were wholeheartedly accepted as kings by the defeated people of every land. The people felt safe about their lives and properties under the Persian rulers. This anomaly can be explained in two words. "Good-Governance". These rulers were religious and believed that immortality could be attained only through a wise, just and holy rule. Although their history began with Cyrus's conquering much of the Assyrean empire but he laid the tradition of a benevolent and respectable conqueror and not a ruthless destroyer. The Persian kings brought peace and prosperity to the people for 200 hundred years. The efficiency of their political administration was comparable to none until the Roman Empire came to power. They would preserve the cultures of the defeated kingdoms also and treat them respectably. And so it was not difficult to bring innumerable kingdoms under the Persian hegemony. This was a very great contribution to the history of political values for the later governments to come. This gave rise to the concept of cosmopolitanism. They brought together various civilizations and developed a new kind of culture where all were free to live their lives according to their own values. Even today the biggest dream of the political philosophies is also the same. The dream of forming a world government. To stay together, yet to preserve one's own culture.

The zenith of the accomplishments of these early kinds of empires is seen in the next era of civilizations. It is termed as classical civilization because man reached almost a stage of perfection. And it was after this civilization that a steady decline was seen in the art of governance after this era. The most classic civilizations of this stage are the early Europeans, the Greek, the Early Roman, the Indian, the Chinese and the ancient Americans.

To begin with in this sequence, are the early Europeans, who were a warrior class. They lived in temporary villages and good governance for them was, to engage in continuous warfare. The interesting fact about them is that they all are Asiatic in their origin. The people from Asia Minor crossed to Greece, Belgrade, Bohemia, Rhine-land and Northern France. Then there were the Indo-European people who reached Europe via Iran and Mesopotamia. They reached Central Europe via South Russia, defeated people living there, and settled in Poland, Silesia, Baveria and Scandinavia. The Celts, the Germans, they all were early Europeans who faced a lot of destruction as they came from other places and had to fight for a right to stay on. So, to continue warfare was their necessity and good governance had no meaning for them.

Next in the sequence was the Greek-civilization. The Greeks considered their leaders as demigods and themselves as the direct descendent of God. Each city-state had its own patron god or goddess. Therefore the Greek felt they had a common parentage and a common bond. But ironically they could never organize themselves into a united centrally governed state. This became their biggest flaw and the Romans as well as the Macedonians took advantage of it. They lost their independence as well as their political institutions. But the world could never forget their political philosophies and ideas of governance. Those ideas that they themselves could not put to practice, ever, have become the harbingers of all coming philosophers. Till date, no other ideology could succeed in dismantling the Greek system of democracy and individual freedom! They were utopians, thinkers and abstract speculators. Even wage labor in their opinion restricted the path to free choice in life. They asserted that individual was neither created for obeying the rulers to gratify their fantasies nor was he a toy for the god. The individual had a right upon his own life, to lead a good life and the measure of good governance was none other than the individual's progress. Even the tyrants worked for the upliftment of the subjects. They defended people's rights. In 621 B.C., Draco, a tyrant, gave the first written law to the people. All the citizens got the right to be tried before a jury before being sentenced or punished. This was an everlasting tribute to the human heritage!

The Greek era is replete with such examples where the citizen were for the first time taken as the focal point of creating as well as testing 'good governance'. Solon, the tyrant, gave us the first written constitution, and himself went into exile to let his constitution be implemented without his interference, in a fair manner. It was such an example of righteousness that was never ever repeated in the history of governance. He gave all the people a voice in the political functioning of the state. Later Cleisthenses further improved upon this idea and stopped voting frauds of clans and kinship, giving voting rights to all, on the basis of geographical sections. All became equal before law for the first time. He also introduced a system of ostracism in which citizens were asked to write the name of those persons in the government whom they considered dangerous for themselves or for the city. If many people criticized a man he was put behind the bars for a least ten years. It is really surprising that a, so called tyrant gave a final decisive right to the common man, paving the way to the tradition of citizen's sovereignty so long ago. While not even the largest democracies of the world, are prepared to give the right to recall to its citizens, even today. The Greek philosopher protagoras, in 4th century B.C. declared citizen as the measure of good governance. The drawback was that they were matchlessly imaginative, but weak planners. And thus they could never achieve good governance.

Then came the Roman Empire, with kings enjoying limitless powers. But they consulted all the heads of clans before taking crucial decisions. These heads together formed a council of elders. The kings also had popular assemblies, called as Comitia Curiata. They could vote, in-groups, but could not form laws. This mightiest empire of antiquity also lost its powers to the nobles of the land. And for five hundred years after that, a republican form of government existed in Rome. It had consuls, tribunes, quaestors, and praetors to assist the plebeians and patricians to govern the state with the help of the 'great Roman law'. These Republics soon degeneratd because they lacked centralization. They began to appoint military dictators that ultimately again led to the establishment of monarchies. The story of decline and fall of Roman Empire brings to the fore three facts about political institutions. One is that they are always in a flux, two, that the established nobility of anytime always brings imbalance in the existing forms of governance, to get a better deal in the changed one. The third fact is that it is always the apathy, lack of interest and lack of patriotism of the common man, in the state and its affairs, which brings the downfall of political institutions and governments. That is why the meaning of good governance always keeps on changing! It is always in a flux!

When we begin to study the early Indian civilization in the sequence of classical civilizations, its history of political institutions and governance is mostly to be traced in the religious scriptures found here. Tribal chieftains existed in early periods. Priest occupied important political positions and even led the armies to war. Yajnavalkya's and Siddhartha' philosophies later helped kings to unite their people. Chandragupta, Ashoka and the Gupta encouraged the people to work on medicine, astronomy, arts and literature. They did not tamper with the growth of their culture and civilization. Later, Mongolians came and with it the history of steady progress of Indian people suddenly changed. For a century, India was governed off and on by invaders. These were cruel ruthless despots. They hurt and destroyed the common man's economy, growth and culture. It was only when king Harsha came back to power that things changed. But great harm was already done in the process. The military, oppressive dictatorship of the Mohammedans turned the impoverished and insulted Indian people towards religion and a belief in rebirth. To sooth their ego they took refuge in supernatural consolations. They began to believe that life on earth was very short, so freedom of body and soul from earthly bondage became their priority. Thus customs became more important than civic laws. Criminals were branded as evil spirits. The civilization became more religious. Science was also used to supplement it Astronomy, grammar and philosophy all of them were used to explain and propagate religion. The princes controlled the people with help from the priests and from the warriors. The whole of India was never centralized in the Oriental or the classical times. But there were absolute monarchies, which controlled the people. On the other hand the only purpose of the people was to attain moksha (salvation). Our classical epics talk of great monarchs, religious monarchs, and warrior monarchs, monarchs and monarchies all the way. The tribals, the feudals, the lords, the priests, the warriors, all of them aspired to become kings, to rule over the people and the land. The history of political development of the entire world shows this pattern. So till recent years good governance meant good kingdoms, strong kings and obedient and faithful subjects! If we analyze very deeply, this urge is still there in every head of the government of the world. It is suppressed due to the latest ideal of democracy, which no administrator can openly deny in the present world of human rights and fundamental rights. Otherwise, all wish to wield unlimited powers.

Equally oriental & classical was the history of Chinese civilization. It had thirteen celestial emperors who reigned for eighteen thousand years. China also started it history of governance with mythological rulers, like Fu-His and Shen-Nung. They taught the people the arts of life, agriculture, commerce, science of medicine, the wheel, the compass, the calendar and house building. The kings were believed to be divine rulers appointed in heaven. And they also played the role of priests. But the people had the powers to dethrone them if they did not help them to develop and prosper. The public administrators were appointed on their merits, skills and intelligence. The emperors sacrificed for the public in many ways and set ideals before them to follow, such as, they would starve during famines along with their subjects although sufficient food would be there in the palace for him. Yet, even such benevolent kings were removed and their good governance was rejected not by the people but by the powerful noble men. These nobles first divided the kingdoms amongst themselves. And then fought with each other to suppress any one from amongst them, who would try to rise. This continued till the peace loving emperors of Hans dynasty took over. The people prospered, learning was encouraged, military expenditures were reduced, penal code was reformed, uniform taxation was introduced, and the middle class elite were pampered and promoted on the basis of their accomplishments. Arts, literature, poetry, mathematics and medicine were encouraged and developed. The Chinese still proudly call themselves the sons of Hans Dynasty. It was their golden period. This was stopped and the heaven on earth was lost by the invasion of barbarians. As always a progressing society was not a cause for stability, because good governance for the people was never good governance for the noble class! Again the wheel went a full circle, and able kings of the Tang and Sung dynasties arose. They enacted civil-service laws, on the basis of Confucian principles. The kings were remarkable administrators. One of them Wang An Shih (1021-1086) is on records for defining a good governance in the following words, "The state should take the entire management of commerce, industry and agriculture in its own hands to prevent the rich from grounding the poor working class to dust". Again the jealous and conservative noble class rose in opposition. In 1279, therefore, the last prince of Sung dynasty was murdered and the Mongols enslaved China.

The last in the sequence of classical civilizations were the ancient civilizations of America. Their political institutions are not available in many records in details, for us to study. The Mexicans, the Mayans and the Incas have some archeological remains, which tell us something about their societies and governance. Their societies were sharply divided between the upper classes and the lower classes. The lower classes were total slaves who had no rights of their own. They were the maimed subjects of the upper classes. The priests and the privileged classes took even their personal lives' decisions. Mostly loosely organized governments ruled, with occasional coming up of some emperors here or there. So law was completely in the hands of the higher classes. This weak government structure was of great convenience to the European invaders who came later on to seize power, and established a large and powerful United State of America.

Coming to the middle age, the harbinger of the modern age, it is accepted as the most important stage of the development of such institutions of governance, which became the founding stones of present day political systems. The Germans, the Christians, the Byzantiums, the Persians, The Arabics, the Moslems, the Mongolians, the Europeans, all together gave rise to the following factors in the concept of modern governance.

Rise of individualism: Rise in the common man's role in the governance of his state.

Rise of nationalism: Rise in the common man's role in the preservation of his state.

Rise of middle class: Rise in the role of elite as well as average middle class masses in the formation of governments of their states.

The entire span of middle age has been an untiring effort of the middle class to assert its identity before the traditional wielder of power, may they be kings, or feudal lords or religious priests. Therefore at that time, good governance was measured by the opportunity given to the middle class to take part in the act of governance. This opportunity was scarcely allowed. That is why Middle Ages are termed as the dark-ages by the intellectual elite.

Renaissance and reformation brought the dawn of modern systems of governance but not without much bloodshed and anarchy. The French revolution, the Russian revolution, the Fascist Italy, the Nazi Germany, the dictatorial Japan, the Great Napoleon, all of them brought to the fore such men who were the elite and the intellectuals from the middle class. They captured power in the name of the common man, the individual, and the masses and utilized it for their own good. They sent uncountable loads of this common man to the mouths of the cannons in the name of nationalism. Hitler rightly and honestly called them 'cannon fodder'. This word nationalism has been exploited sometimes in the name of fascism, sometimes in the name of communism, sometimes in the name of liberalism, still on other times in the name of socialism. These elite and neo-powerful leaders sometimes used the representative form of government, sometimes the Parliament form of Government and sometimes the Presidential Form of Government to woo the common man to vote for their elevation to power. The common man is still common. There has been no elevation for him ever!

Good governance is that which delivers the goods to the common man. But it has been proved here beyond doubt that good governance is every thing other than that. Some times it is the fanatic craze of an emperor or a dictator to own the whole world, and the common man goes crazy in fulfilling his king's desire by even sacrificing his own life for it. Some times it is the pampered craving of the nobility to add yet more feathers to its cap and the common man is honestly fooled to attain it for them in the name of caste, religion, community and group loyalties. And most painfully, at other times it is the idealistic whim of the intellectual class to see its 'common-man-welfare' theory put to practice and the common man marches on, in full faith, to revolt for the revolutionary's revolution! And the game goes on but the welfare is missing.

Another fact that has come to the fore, after going through the history of the chain of governance right from the pre-literate man to the present is that: kinds of governments do not necessarily decide the quality of governance. A monarch, a religious or military dictator both may be benevolent towards their subjects. They may help them in their welfare and save them from their enemies. And the masses have shown willful voluntary and absolute obeisance towards such totalitarian monarchs. They have been proud of being their subjects. The question of their right to sovereignty and their right to take part in the governance of their state never arose in their minds.

Does this not give rise to the doubt that the entire theory of rights, natural or fundamental, was the brain child of the middle class elite, who could never attain the power of governance in their own hands due to lack of human support and material power, with them? And that the common man never aspired for them or kept them as his first priority as long as his basic needs were being fulfilled.

Now that the whole world is crying for the implementation, for the restoration and for the realization of democratic rights, human rights, fundamental rights and so many other rights, the common man is all the more confused, perplexed and bewildered! He wonders he is getting so many things in writing, but the basic necessities are still no where in sight. He is amazed that he is now a sovereign, as powerful as a king, but he is still not able to locate his own human dignity. The catastrophe becomes all the more glaring because of the mass media's worldwide propaganda of the facilities that could be availed by man by the use of science and technology. This situation is all the more pitiable for the educated common man because he is still more aware of his helpless and hopeless plight.

The educated common man has now known that empires were built, wars were fought, and civilizations and cultures were formed at the grave of his martyrdom. He was the Christ who was always crucified at the altar of so many isms, worldly or holy! The talk of human rights, was always a sham! And so the entire world now is in a restless flux of dissatisfaction. The common man no more wants to play puppet in the hands of the neo-rich, the neo-lords, the neo-kings, the neo-politicians the neo-bureaucrats, in the name of good governance! This, thus, is a dangerously reactionary phase, where people seem to explode at the slightest instigation, especially in states where there is scarcity of even minimum resources of living.

'Now he knows that good governance is a metaphorical dichotomy of these two words because governance has never been good for him, and may never be good in future too! The word GOVERNANCE, unless replaced by the word MANAGEMENT can never be good. It will always keep reminding him of past oppression, serfdom and slavery of the ruled by the rulers. Its expectations will remain only hypothetically euphorial unless the word-organized management replaces good governance. Its reality will always have to depend upon oligarchic myrmidons if good governance does not transform into the common man's participatory politics. Its prospects will always be 'conditionally tergiversational' and 'ephemeral' if the ultimate nature and universal psychology of the human being is not understood properly. And that is "Any government of state, any king or dictator, any war lord or divine leader, any parliament or council and any Prime Minister or President can be adjudged as not only good, excellent if it helps the two basic urges of the citizens to be fulfilled. One, is his search for truth and the second is his quest for happiness, History has proved this fact. This paper corroborates it with sufficient examples. Humanity progressed, science developed, nations prospered and peace & harmony prevailed only when the ordinary human being was allowed a free hand in the satisfaction of his curiosities, and attainment of his happiness even under absolute monarchies and aristocracies. That this can happen only under a true democracy, is a subject of serious introspection.

References

Thorndike, L., *History of Civilization* (1926).

Barnes, H.E., *The History of Western Civilization* (1935).

Blackmar, F.W., *History of Human Society* (1926).

Schneider, H., *The History of World Civilizations from Prehistoric-Time to the Middle Ages* (1931).

Cambridge History of India (Macmillan 1922).

Adams G.B., *Civilization during the Middle Ages* (1922).

Cheyney, E.P., *The Dawn of a New Era* (1936).

Benes, E., *Democracy: Today and Tomorrow* (1939).

Dewey, J. & others, *Living Philosophies* (1931).

3

Good Governance: An Overview

S. K. Chaturvedi

In post second Great War a number of Afro-Asian countries got themselves liberated from colonial and imperial yoke with a hope that it would be possible for them to ensure a better life to their people. However, dearth of technological know-how and trained man power, absence of stable political system, process of political development and intensified cold war scenario compelled them to seek economic, technological and strategic assistance from the developed countries. In the closing decades of the twentieth century the aid-giving countries, while taking a stock of the development of third world countries coined concepts like modernization, development, competitive economy, rule of law, application of human rights etc, as yardstick for such evaluation. 'Good Governance' was one amongst such parameter evolved by the western world very recently. Development assistance to the third world countries in the Post Cold War era has thus been subject to the new politics of 'Good Governance'. In 1989 the concept of good governance was for the first time highlighted in the World Bank document on Sub-Saharan Africa.

The document mentioned 'Improving Governance would begin with an assessment of the institutional environment, with emphasis on the key governance elements of accountability, rule of law, openness and transparency which determines the patrimonial profile of the country....'. Thus, four parameters were laid down by the document for assessing the standard of governance of a country. Obviously if a country is high on the above four point matrix the same may be bracketed as 'good'. At this stage it seems appropriate to ponder over whether good governance as defined by the above mentioned document is appropriate or what should be the parameters for terming the governance as 'good'.

Etymologically, Governance stands for 'rule with authority', conduct of policy or affair'. In democracy authority rests in people, hence governance is linked with the consent of people and obviously for the good of people. The British council subscribes this view by stating that governance refers to a process whereby elements in society wield power, authority and influence and enact policies and discussion concerning public life and social upliftment', *i.e,.,* a governance is good when it is in the larger interest of the masses. The World Bank amongst other factors identified, rule of law and transparency as the yardstick for evaluating good governance. World bank's document entitled 'Governance and Development (1992) put it as the manner in which power is exercised in the management of a country's economic and social resources for development. Further good governance is 'creating and sustaining an environment which fastens strong and equitable development. The document underlined political regime, which is a process by which authority is exercised in the management of country's economic and social resources and capacity of government to implement policies, as the parameters to assess the quantum of good governance. Thus philosophically speaking the objective of good governance is to convert the bad and nasty society into an orderly and peace keeping one as accepted by the great contractual thinker Hobbes. Obviously, good governance has different meaning for the scholars. If for Pai Panandhikar good governance is a process, which leads its people to a peaceful, orderly, reasonable, prosperous and participatory lives, for others good governance is identified by political accountability and transparency in respect of dissemination of information and cooperation between government and society. In other words, good governance denotes a citizen friendly, citizen caring, responsive and transparent system capable of the promotion, preservation and protection of the human rights of the citizens. The World Bank Report has summarized the above view points by identifying the characteristics of the good governance as a government which is politically accountable, a society where people are law abiding, where freedom is available to them, and bureaucracy is accountable to the people, transparency is maintained in the dissemination of information, administration is efficient, effective and responsive to the society and the government and society stand in a cooperative way. In fine, good governance is that which suits to the aspirations and ethos of the people and those selected for operating the system should be endowed with character and competence and are motivated by the spirit of service to the people in true sense. OECD countries have summarized the concept of good governance by identifying its essentials as ensuring democratization of the system while confirming people's participation in the process of development, preservation and protection of Human Rights of each individual. Thus, an equitable, transparent, non-discriminatory, socially sensitive, and accountable administration having capability and highly organized effectiveness which can achieve such goal are the requirements for good governance.

In our country the conference of chief secretary's (1996) while discussing the concept admitted that public administration and civil services in India is passing through a crises period due to eroded capability and effectiveness of civil service, nexus of politician, bureaucracy and even criminals, low level of honesty and transparency and non-accessibility of the political elements and bureaucracy, accountable for ensuring an effective administration, to the people. In other words, an efficient, open, transparent responsive, accountable, clean, dynamic, result oriented administration is necessary towards ensuring good governance. Out of these transparency, accountability, and administrative reforms at all levels and in all sectors seem to be the crux of the issue.

To be more specific whereas accountability is holding the government functionaries and organizations responsible for performance, action and inaction transparency denotes governmental functioning in openness as much as possible as well as citizens rights to know about the government's transaction. It may not be out of place to mention here that the goals of accountability can only be achieved with a wide-ranging people's participation *i.e*,.. people acting as watch dog over government's activities and use of national resources so as to determine the ability and efficiency of public services. Needless to mention that continuous process of administrative reforms need to be adhered for keeping the administrative machinery galvanized and efficient.

At this stage it becomes relevant to evaluate attempts made by the government to achieve the twin goals of accountability and transparency. As defined by the webster's's New International Dictionary of English language, the term accountability has been defined as to 'render account', obviously before any person, authority or institution. In a democratic system since people are sovereign hence, the political and administrative system is to render its account' before the people by making them aware about the objective, structure, function of administrative organization, formulation of policies, its implementations and achievement etc. Obviously, it is possible only in a transparent system. Government of India in this context has framed a plan for making and keeping the administration accountable and transparent. It declares that time has come for a strong message to be conveyed that administration is for people and to make it sure that the government intends to frame citizens charter, lay down time limits and standards for services and avenues of grievance redressal, for the reason that the foremost test to good governance is the degree of 'Public satisfaction' and easy accessibility of the people to the channels of grievance redressal so as to get the problems settled down being faced by them. The broad principles of such charter are that wide publicity of standards of performance of public agencies and local bodies be ensured, assurance of quality of service, courtesy and helpfulness of staff, choice and consultation with the citizens, simplified and convenient procedure of receipt of complaints and their time bound redressal and independent scrutiny of performance of the administration with the help of group of citizens should be ensured so as to fulfil the commitments made to the people by the government of the day. The measures so initiated need to be brought to the notice of all concerned and common people. Such steps may be helpful in making the system accountable.

The public grievances primarily arise out of the inaccessibility of officials, failure even to acknowledge applications, non-enforcement of any kind of time limits about the job entrusted to the agencies and unsympathetic attitude of officials towards people at various levels. Necessary steps may be taken to project that the system is sensitive to the people's problems. In this context at the very out set, arrangements need to be made to a friendly welcome of the complainant by providing him physical facilities and basic information alongwith initiating a time bound redressal mechanism.

The 73rd and 74th amendment of the constitution has chartered a path in realizing the dream of responsive government. Need of time is to strengthen the grass root institutions financially and administratively. Needless to mention that in a democratic system the administration is required to be accountable to the people sitting at all levels, for which if need be, new laws should be enacted, regulations framed and procedure made simpler and transparent so as the interest of weaker and poorer section of the society may be served.

Secrecy and lack of openness is the symbol of a feudal and authoritarian administrative system. A responsive system needs to be open and transparent so as to ensure people's trust in the governance and minimizing the level of corruption. For transparent system accessibility to information about decisions relating to public affairs need to be ensured for which an appropriate procedure need to be laid down for easy accessibility to concerned government records and papers. Law may be enacted or amended in respect of official secret Act. It may be relevant to note here that often people are not interested in seeking the information but the very provision that such information may be extracted from the government may help in building people's trust in the system of governance. However, for such a governance the very structure of government and processes is required to be improved by making rules for negating the unwanted political interference in the system, ensuring codification and simplification of procedures and taking citizen friendly initiatives. Further as tenth plan paper envisages, peoples participation at all stages of planning, implementation and monitoring and democratic decentralization is required to be taken to accelerate the socio-economic development with in a participatory framework at the grass root level, civil service reforms need to be initiated by minimizing discretion, revamping of the system may be taken up by stream lining procedure of reward and punishment, induction of professionals and specialists in the administration, training for capacity and capability building, procedural reforms covering all aspects of government, interface with the public, judicial reforms for speeding up the process of delivering justice and using information technology for improving efficiency, transparency and making interface with government. Good governance is the corner stone of any democratic system for which each and every one right from man in street to persons in parliament must remain vigilant and put their best of efforts to realize the very objective of the constitution. Bata K. Dey has rightly mentioned 'Government, after all is a tryst with trust, a commitment of people for the people, a social compact for the greatest good, the collective conscience of the community. It is not the handiwork of way ward politicians or handmaiden bureaucrats, or the property of unscrupulous handfuls who manipulate majority at majority's cost. People must have a stake in the government for people have a stake in their future. Future is the place where all of us will live the rest of our lives.

The parameters evolved by the developed countries for evaluating the intensity of good governance of development countries are always not applicable in their case because of the environmental compulsions. The real assessment of good governance seem to be is whether the people are satisfied with the system of governance and if so goodness of the governance is vouch safe.

References

1. Mohit Bhattacharya, Conceptualizing Good Governance, *IJPA*, p. 291.
2. Action plan or for an Effective Government, Deptt. of Administrative, Ministry of personnel reforms and Public Grievances, Govt. of India, New Delhi.
3. Mohit Bhattacharya, Conceptualizing Good Governance, *IJPA*, Vol. XLIV, No.3, 1998.
4. R.S. Tiwari, Good Governance, *IJPA*, Vol. XLVIII, No. 4, 2002.
5. Bata K. Dey, Defining Good Governance, *IJPA*, Vol. XLIV, No.3 1996.
6. C.P. Barthwal, E-Governance, *IJPA*, Vol. 64, No. 3-4, 2003.

4

Socio-Political Aspects of Good Governance

S. N. Singh

Ever since state came into existence, governance has been an issue of concern for the social scientists world over. Aristotle's familiar observation that 'state came into existence for life, but continues to exist for good life' is a theme of continual relevance which can hardly be ignored or denied. In the Indian context, doubts have been expressed about the system of governance which some may feel that of date it has become a casualty. Successive governments have been promising good governance on the eve of election but some how have yet to fulfil the promise. Under the circumstances, it has raised a debate in the country. The present paper attempts to analyse the socio-political aspect of good governance. The paper is divided into three broad heads viz, the background, parameter and lastly the factors affecting and for good governance.

Background

India opted for a political structure which in a sense had little roots in its societal framework and the value frame. Looking at the social order that India persisted with for centuries is one marked with heterogeneity and inequality. Further, during the later period, we come across a caste based social system. This caste based social system operated for quite a long period and influenced other aspects of political and administrative system. The post independence India was deliberately designed to different from its historical past by focusing on new value frame suited to new Political system. During the freedom struggle, there was focus on self- governance and between the choice of 'good governance' and 'self government' primacy was attached to self government. It was the question of attaining freedom from foreign rule and bondage. It was a struggle against oppression of various kinds. In view of the importance and urgency of this freedom, other aspects got sidelined.

India got independence on 15th of August, 1947 through a transfer of power from the British to Indian Government. Following this, an interim government took over and a Constituent Assembly was constituted to frame a constitution for India. The constitution thus formulated was adopted on 1949 by the people of India. The Preamble of the Constitution of India thus provides the basic premise for future governance. It is worth noting the contents of the Preamble for the purpose of our analysis. It says that:

"We, the people of India..."

The Preamble thus clearly indicates the nature of the polity and the socioeconomic system that the future India is going to have. Also emerging from it is the nature and the role of governance. Precisely, the concept of democracy, socialism and secularism and the philosophies which would determine the system of governance of future India. After the attainment of self government at the national level, the need for good governance has also come on the agenda of various political parties in the country. For sometime now, there is a realisation on the part of political parties that governance has suffered some where down the line. In view of this, perhaps the last couple of general elections have witnessed the emergence of the slogan of good governance. For in the absence of good governance, the very relevance and continuance of such governance is questioned.

The issue of good governance basically emerges from the good socio-political environment. There is an inter-dependence of socio-political and administrative system as they operate in wider environment. The present concern for good governance emerges from the widespread problems which have been influencing the politics. For the last two - three general elections, there is an emergence of coalition of political parties as no single political party is able to secure majority in the Parliament. Gradually, one observes that the days of one party dominant system seems to be over and a system based on a coalition of parties is replacing that. Sometimes, the coalition is pre-poll and often it may be post-poll. There would, therefore, be a difference in two types of system.

The socio-political process over the years has witnessed several changes at different levels including policy. To illustrate, one would like to analyse the role of caste in our social and political system, there is no denying the fact that caste has continued to play an increasing role in the socio-political process. Several governments during the last few decades have granted reservations in political as well as administrative positions. The electoral process too has been continuously influenced by these factors irrespective of political outfit. Under such circumstances, societal fragmentation has taken place which gets reflected in various forms and at various levels. The fragmentation has reached to such an extent that there is clear cut division of vote on these bases. This division influences the electoral process which leads to division of votes and diversification of parties.

Moreover, the political process lacks serious ideological grounding and base. For the last fifty years of political process in India would provide the testimony for the observation. Whether one party dominant system or a multi-party coalition, it has functioned more on personal basis than any thing else. The national parties like the Indian National Congress has depended more on the Nehru family than on any political ideology. Even the Communist parties, at times, become victim of such a personality basis and orientation. The parties like AIADMK, SP, BSP, TDP etc. are depending more on their party chief rather than any ideological commitment. People have left one party, formed or joined some other, not because of any ideological, but because of personal factors. The Indian political system, therefore, has had a hollow ideological base which got reflected in the conduct of proceedings at different levels.

The Indian socio-political order, therefore, apart from being heterogeneous, has based itself more on persons and individuals than ideology or rationality. This has given rise to a system where governance became rather complex and difficult.

II. Parameters

There could be several parameters for the analysis of good governance. However, we would like to confine the discussion on two broad areas which concern the people at large. As such, we have identified the following two areas for the purposes of discussion here

(a) Administration of Justice- Regulatory Administration.

(b) Administering Development- Development Function.

(a) Administering Justice

Under this head, we would try to analyse the question of law and order, administration of justice and other regulatory functions of the government and s how far it has been able to govern and deliver.

The situation on the law and order front has not been very encouraging during all these periods. Cases of deteriorating law and order situation has kept bothering several state governments including Uttar Pradesh. There seems to be no respite from deteriorating law and order situation as cases of murder, dacoity, loot, theft etc. have continued to bother general public, on the one hand people are bothered by the ant-social elements and mafias on the other, the machinery responsible for maintenance of law and order has not been very efficient for various reasons. Many a times, in order to show the lower rate of crime and improving law and order situation, the crime is often not properly recorded. Non-reporting of crime is often resorted to by the administration in order to show a better law and order situation. This considerably influences governance and raises serious doubts over the intention as well as the capability of the administration to handle such situation. The inadequacy can be identified in all the three areas of the administration viz. structure, the process and the behaviour.

The administration responsible for law and order and the machinery engaged in this sphere is more akin to colonial administration rather than to modern Indian administration. The rules, regulations, the laws are centuries old when the entire gamut of administration was different. The objectives were different, the method too was supposed to be different. The nature of governance was supposed to be different then what it is today. The anticipated change in the structure, process and behaviour could not take place as was desired. The consequent impact of this has been the inefficient and non-responsive administration. The custodial death further raise serious doubt on the efficacy and the accountability of our administration. In a democratic system of governance, such situations do not explain the validity of good governance.

(b) Administering Development

The other parameter on which one would like to examine the question of good governance is that of growth and development. The rationale being that a good governance should reflect in socio-economic growth and development. In this context, the question to be analysed is that of poverty alleviation, employment generation, increase in goods and services provided to the poor, both in rural as well as urban sectors. Also, the growth registered in various agro-industrial as well as service and other sectors.

As we are all aware India opted for planning as a tool of development. It deliberately opted for planned development instead of unplanned one. To meet the requirement of these planned effort, the Planning Commission at the Government of India was created with Prime Minister as its ex-officio Chairman and a full time Deputy Chairman along with several members and subject specialists. At the state level too State Planning Boards were created for the preparation and monitoring of plans. The First Five Year Plan was, thus launched in the year 1952. Since then, nine Five Year Plans and two Annual Plans have been launched in the country and the tenth one is on. It has, therefore, been almost five decades of planned development in the country which should generally be reflected in the development sector.

It may be noted here that there is no derth of data and information on this aspect of governance. Several studies by the government agencies as well as non-governmental and autonomous ones have reported growth in different sectors of the economy. The agricultural sector has reported increase in production so much so that the country is in surplus so far as the food-grain is concerned. The Green Revolution, the White Revolution all go to prove that the economy has recorded growth during the last fifty years of planned effort. Similarly, in the industrial sector too, there is adequate data to prove that India has recorded growth in the industrial sector as well. However, in spite of the growth in the economy, inequality has persisted. The problem like poverty, unemployment, illiteracy, hunger have continued to bother the policy planners. The latest World Bank Report has opined that the gap between the rich and the poor has increased. Mahbub-ul-Haque[1] has argued that the poverty in the third world countries has increased in spite of development efforts. The poor have become poorer and the rich, richer due to development in these countries. He has argued that this reported growth is without justice and hence, he has termed it as a 'sin'. This raises a question mark on nature of the strategy for development as well as the quality of governance. It becomes difficult to explain the surplus stock of food grain on the face of starvation and abject poverty.

The question of governance on the two parameters referred to earlier would explain the nature and quality of governance. In view of the available data and information, it may be difficult to term the contemporary system of governance as good governance.

III. Factors Affecting Good Governance

A number of factors have been identified by the scholars for good governance. Some of the important ones are being identified here for the purpose of analysis.

(a) Rule of Law
(b) Literacy/Education
(c) Controlling Corruption
(d) Living within means
(e) Effective Reward and Punishment
(f) Development of Human Resource
(g) Gap between Precept and Practice should be minimal

These are some of the areas which deserve special consideration in the analysis of socio-political factors affecting good governance in the country. This is not to suggest that these are the only areas, but these factors do deserve special attention of the powers that be and other sections of the society. In the absence of these, the achievement of good governance would be difficult. We can analyse each of these seven factors separately and see how deeply these are influencing the good governance in the country.

One would agree that the main basis of democratic government in the country is the rule of law. However, there is enough data to support that it is the rule of persons rather than that of the rule of the law. People feel proud in defying the law with vengeance. Under the circumstances, the socio-political system throws negative signal for proper governance.

Even after fifty years of planned development, the country is still not literate. Majority of the population living in rural areas continues to be illiterate and uneducated. Under such social indicators, it is rather difficult to achieve the good governance.

Another factor affecting good governance is that of corruption. As a matter of fact, corruption has become wide spread and has influenced considerably the socio-political process which hampers good governance. Therefore, controlling corruption is an important factor for achieving good governance.

There is tendency amongst different groups of living beyond means. Due to scientific advancement and the technological development, the society is exposed to new facts. There is temptation to become rich that too unjustifiably lesser period gives rise to this tendency. The Chief Vigilance Commissioner's latest figure is around 2000 such cases unless the tendency is checked it would be difficult to provide good governance.

For good governance it is important to have a good reward and punishment system. Somehow, the Indian administrative system don't show to have one. In the absence of good reward and punishment system, inefficiency and mediocrity prevails which can not pass for good governance.

One of the new areas for good governance is concerned with development of human resources. The government of India realising the importance of Human Resource sometimes back changed the name of Education Ministry to Human Resource Development Ministry ensuring a wider coverage. But only change in the nomenclature is not going to help much unless there are major policy changes in this sector.

Last factor which could be considered in this context is related with the question of a gap persisting between what we say and practise. There will be high sounding policy declaration on the one hand and on the other there is no practice of the same. In view of this gap, the credibility of the government remains at stake which can not be considered vital for good governance.

These are some of the factors affecting good governance. We have not tried to burden the paper with data as these issues are of common knowledge and perception. In order, therefore, to achieve good governance, these factors have to be controlled.

References

1. Mahbub-ul-Haque, *The Poverty Curtain*, Choices for the Third World.

5

Good Governance: The Question of Reviewing the Constitution

S. K. Jha

Sanctity of the Constitution

With India's fairly long spell of democratic governance, there comes a new experiment in constitutionalism, the politics of constitutional review. Under the democratic rule the constitution is considered to be sacred document. The party in power is not supposed to interfere with it arbitrarily to further its own political interest. Nevertheless, every constitution contains provisions for either incorporating in it or deleting from it certain provisions in the larger interest of governance or the changing needs of the nation. This kind of sanctity of the constitution, in fact, ensures the successful functioning of democracy and also the development of the polity.

Merit of the Indian Constitution

India even before independence had made clear its ambition and determination to go in for a democratic governance after attainment of freedom. In order to achieve this goal she undertook proper and suitable measures to draft and adopt a constitution on the eve of its independence. The constitution which it finally adopted drew heavily from the experiences of democratic governance in the west under various and different constitutional principles and practices. Nevertheless, the Indian constitution received high praise from constitutional pundits both from within and without the country. E. Barker, an eminent British Political Scientist and a constitutional expert, paid laurels to the framers of the constitution for working out a magnificent Preamble. At the time of emergence of the India Republic Sir Anthony Eden, The Prime Minister of Britain had said:

"Of all the experiments in government, which have been attempted since the beginning of time. I believe that the Indian venture into parliamentary government is the most exciting. A vast subcontinent is attempting to apply to tens and thousands of millions a system of free democracy...It is a brave thing to try to do so. The Indian venture is not a pale imitation of out practice at home, but a magnified and multiplied reproduction on a scale we have never dreamt of. If it succeeds, its influence on Asia is incalculable for good. Whatever the outcome, we must honour those who attempt it."[1]

Even more exalting was the opinion expressed by an American authority, Granville Austin who wrote that what the Indian Constituent Assembly began was "perhaps the greatest political venture since that originated in Philadelphia in 1787."[2] He further described the Indian Constitution as "first and foremost a social document." The majority of India's constitutional provisions are either directly arrived at furthering the aim of social revolution or attempt to foster this revolution by establishing conditions necessary for its achievement.[3]

The very point was elaborated in eloquent terms by Ambedkar and Nehru who maintained: "what makes our constitution relevant to the conditions and the problems of India and the developing world is, in fact, the socio-economic soul of it. Its uniqueness is that it has combined this harmoniously with the liberal rights and freedoms as conceived by the western democracies."[4]

At the final stage of the constitution making Dr. B. R. Ambedkar called it one of the finest constitutions in the world. Highlighting the significance of the fundamental rights incorporated in the constitution he had also asserted:

"The Declaration of the Rights of Man....has become part and parcel of our mental make-up.....These principles have become the silent, immaculate premise of our outlook."

While democratic experiments and constitutions have failed in many of the Afro-Asian countries, the Indian constitution has stood the test of time and survived any by a large worked well for more than half a century. Although it was not tailored to be a thoroughly flexible constitution, yet it has shown tremendous adaptability to changing situations and the nation's needs. Eighty amendments have been incorporated in it—some very minor and technical while others quite important and vital too. Nevertheless, it has had its failures as well, not on account of its structural defects but perhaps because of the weakness of its operators. The framers had a vision of it.

On the historic day of the beginning of deliberations of the Constituent Assembly on 9 December, 1946, Sachchidananda Sinha, its provisional Chairman, had quoted in his inaugural address the following words of Joseph Story envisioning the world's newest and largest democracy:

> "The structure has been created by architects of consummate skill and fidelity; its foundations are solid; its compartments are beautiful as well as useful; its arrangements are full of wisdom and order; and its defenses are impregnable from without. It has been reared for immortality, if the work of man may justly aspire to such a title. It may, nevertheless, perish in an hour by the folly, or corruption, or negligence of its own keepers. Republics are created...by the virtue, public spirit and intelligence of the citizens. They fall when the wise are banished from the public councils because they dare to be honest, and the profligate are rewarded because they flatter the people in order to betray them."[5]

Dr. Ambedkar had emphatically asserted after the Constitution was adopted: "It is workable, it is flexible and it is strong enough to hold the country together both in peace time and war time. Indeed, if I may say so, if things so wrong under the new constitution, the reason will not be that we had a bad constitution. What we will have to say is that Man is vile."[6]

Speaking in a similar vein, Rajendra Prasad, as President of the Constituent Assembly had stated: *"If the people who are elected are capable men of character and integrity, they should be able to make the best of a defective constitution. If they are lacking in there, the constitution cannot help the country."*[7]

Fallings of the Indian Constitution

These words of the framers were truly prophetic. Years after the working of the Constitution, Nani Palkhivala, an eminent jurist had to say: *"The foundations of the constitution have been shaken by the folly of the people, the corruption of our politicians and the negligence of the elite. In just thirty years, we have reduced the noble process of our Constitution to the level of a carnival, of claptrap, cowardice and chicanery.*[8] And now recently on the occasion of the golden jubilee of the Republic on 27 January 2000 K.R. Narayanan, the President of India, in his address to the lawmakers raised the point: *"whether it is the constitution that has failed us or we have failed the Constitution."*[9]

Muddling and Meddling with the Constitution

There is no denying the fact that the sanctity of the constitution was fully preserved during the Prime Ministership of Jawaharlal Nehru and Lal Bahadur Shastri. Several amendments to the constitution were however made during this period, but no question was raised on their rationale and propriety. They were generally free from the charge of being politically motivated. If there were criticisms, they were directed against their legal flaws and other defects.

Constitution under Indira Gandhi

The Constitution became a deplorable casualty of the rule of Indira Gandhi. Soon after coming into power Mrs. Gandhi faced stiff challenge not only from the opposition parties but also from a strong section of her own party. In fact, the 1967 general election had given a jolt to the Indian National Congress—a monolith in Indian politics till then. For the first time, the party had been dislodged from power in several states and even at the centre its strength was considerably reduced. To strengthen her position vis-a-vis the external and internal opposition, therefore, became the first priority of Mrs. Gandhi. And she did it by adopting and pursuing a radical and progressive policy. Banks were nationalized and privy purse was abolished and for that necessary amendments were made in the constitution. This clicked and as a result the graph of popularity of the Indian National Congress rose perceptibly. But this happy situation could not remain stable for long. There was popular uprising against corruption in general and misrule of the Congress governments in Gujarat and Bihar. The crisis was further complicated when the election of Mrs. Gandhi was set aside by the Allahabad High Court. Mrs. Gandhi tried to overcome the crisis and remain in power despite that adverse judicial pronouncement by resorting the reckless changes in the constitution which ultimately led to the clamping of emergency and the ushering in of a kind of rule based on total disruption of the constitution itself.

Constitution Defiled and Defaced

During the emergency a paper containing "Some Suggestions" for amending the Constitution was mysteriously circulated. It was a typical filler to the people from the government of the day a far-reaching and drastic constitutional changes. It led to a good deal of whispering campaign and controversy. Ultimately the government appointed the Swaran Singh Committee in 1976 which submitted a report recommending an overhauling of the Constitution. This facilitated the passage of the disreputed 42nd amendment of the Constitution which threatened to change its very character. D. D. Basu rightly said that the 42nd Amendment Act was practically a 'revision' of the constitution.[10] It introduced changes in the Preamble. It changed as many as 53 articles and the seventh schedule. As to substantive changes, it sought to change the vital principles underlying the 1949 Constitution. Article 368 was amended providing that a law described as a Constitutional Amendment Act was made completely immune from challenge in a Court of law, either on a procedural or substantive ground. For the first time, a chapter on Fundamental Duties was introduced in order to counteract the sweep of Fundamental Rights. Fundamental Rights were devalued. By expanding the scope of Article 31C, it was provided that a law seeking to implement any of the Directive Principles would be altogether immune from judicial review on the ground of contravention of fundamental rights. This was exactly the reverse of what provided in the 1949 Constitution.

The Wrong Undone

However, when the Janata Party came to power in March 1977 it took step to fulfil its election pledge to undo the extensive mischief done by the 42nd amendment. But it was only partially successful as the party has no majority in the Rajya Sabha. The first attempt of the party viz. the 43rd Amendment Bill (1977) was abortive. Eventually, the 43rd Amendment Act 1977 was passed with the help of Congress (O). However, the attitude of that party later changed and therefore the 45th Amendment Bill (1978) was passed in a truncated shape as the 44th Amendment Act (1978).

BJP's Commitment to Constitutional Change

The National Democratic Alliance (NDA)—a multi-party alliance which is in power at the centre and in which the Bhartiya Janata Party (BJP) is in the leading position had an old predisposition to bring about changes in the Constitution. This was but natural as the BJP and its root organisation, the RSS has had a political philosophy which is not fully compatible with the ideals and ethos of the Indian Constitution. Soon after the making of the constitution Guru Golwalkar had expressed has displeasure on several points. He has emphasized that the Constitution lacked the understanding of basic difference between the nation and the state. A protagonist of a centralized and homogenized state, the high priest of Jan Sangh (the predecessor of the BJP), Deen Dayal Upadhyaya used to repeatedly underline that the Constitution did not recognise and represent Bharat Mata. The party formulated and professed the doctrine of Indianisation and in keeping with that vociferous advocacy of the abrogation of Article 370 of the Constitution which gives special status to Jammu and Kashmir. Although the party was re-christened as the Bhartiya Janata Party later, but it does carry the old legacy and stands committed to all this on account of the tulelage of the RSS over it. Even now, the RSS is the main plank of its political support and strength. Therefore, soon after coming to power, it tried to show its credential as a party committed to Hindutva.

The BJP along with its coalition partners came to power for the first time at the Centre in 1996 but could not retain it for more than 13 days. Again, in 1998 it managed to form the government at the centre, but could not make it durable. This BJP led government was voted out of power after 13 months by just one vote. But even during this brief spell of its rule, the party showed its intent to bring about the long thought-out changes in the Constitution. This was expressed through the President's address to Parliament on 25th March 1998:

> "Fifty years after independence, the time has come to rejuvenate our institutions so that they are strong enough to meet the challenges of the future. The government proposes to do so as well as appoint a commission to review the Constitution."[11]

When the BJP was voted out of power for the second time, it thought it all the more essential for pragmatic consideration to bring about constitutional changes in order to be stable in power. Hence on the eve of the 1999 election for the Lok Sabha, it launched a campaign for stability of the government by re-fixing the term of the Lok Sabha and State Assemblies and a new pattern of vote of no-confidence on the line of the practice in Germany. It further raised the bogey of eligibility of a person of foreign origin to be a contestant for the post of Prime Ministership. This was clearly directed against Mrs. Sonia Gandhi's prospect of becoming the Prime Minister of the country. The BJP however kept its oft-repeated call for abrogation of Article 370 of the constitution in abeyance for the time-being for political expediency as the other constituents of the National Democratic Alliance (NDA) did not favour it. Hence there was a brief reference of the plan to review the constitution in its Election Manifesto (1999). It pledged to appoint a commission not only in the light of experience and development since 1996, but also of the entire post-independence experience.[12]

When the BJP came to power second time, it reiterated its election pledge through the President's speech to Parliament on 25 October 1999 by detailing out some issues to be taken up by the review team on priority basis. The two issues which were specifically highlighted were (i) to have a fixed five year term for the Lok Sabha and State Assemblies and (ii) to replace the present system of no-confidence motion with a constructive vote of no-confidence.[13]

Overview Committee

BJP did considerable homework before taking the final step to announce a Constitution Review Commission. It set up a four-member overview committee. The members of this committee were Mool Chand Sharma, RKP Shankar Das, Vaidlingam and Ghanshyam Singh. The committee recommended review of more than nine key articles of the constitution relating to centre-state relations, council of ministers, executive power of the Union government, powers of the President of India, Lok Pal and Lokayukta.

On the basis of this report the Union Law Ministry prepared a detailed note and circulated it to all cabinet ministers. The note reportedly covered the following eleven areas: (1) Fundamental Rights, Directive Principles of State Policy and Duties of Citizens, (ii) Accountability of public servants and the definition of public servants, (iii) Stable and effective government, (iv) Check speedy system of justice, (v) multi-cultural and plural polity and protection of ministers and uniform civil code, (vi) Centre-State Relations, (vii) Reservation, (viii) Economic reforms, (ix) Amendments to prevent promulgation of emergency, (x) Neutral bureaucracy, (xi) Zones of silence and vagueness and uncertainties were identified in the constitution and more clarity was sought for effective governance. Further, there was reference to the need of one chapter on political parties in the Constitution. Other specific issues mentioned were (i) to examine the feasibility of converting parliamentary system into a presidential one, (ii) to examine the tenure of Lok Sabha to ensure the stability of the central government, (iii) method of choosing Prime Minister, (iv) to adopt new method to move vote of no-confidence.[14]

President—Prime Minister Controversy

The fact that the BJP was seriously contemplating a major change in the constitution had become a matter of concern and criticism in several quarters in the country. That the President of India also shared this became clear even before the government could constitute a commission to this effect. The President's concern was obliquely reflected in the Republic Day-eve address on 25 January 2000. Highlighting the outstanding merit of the Indian Constitution he said:

> "Our thoughts go back to the founding fathers of our constitution whose farsighted vision and arduous labours gave us a constitution which enshrined the traditional concepts of liberty, equality and fraternity adding to them are concept of justice—social, economic and political—and declaring our nation a Sovereign Democratic Republic."[15]

Pointing out to the government accountability to the people and the Executives responsibility to the Parliament as enshrined in our constitution, the President further stated:

> The word 'Republic' is no ordinary word. It is a commitment to the effect that, in our state, supreme power is exercised not by some remote monarch but by the people. It is an affirmation that the wielder of power in India—the *adhinayaka*—is the great aggregation of out people as a whole...We can be grateful to be the citizens of this Republic where an individual, be he ever so high, the Constitution and the laws made by the people remain higher

than him; and where the Executive remains accountable to the Parliament."[16]

President's opposition to the BJP's plan for the review of the constitution became very bitter and frontal in his speech in the Central Hall of Parliament to mark the Golden Jubilee of India's Republic and the Constitution on 27 January 2000. It is pertinent to note that on that very occasion the Prime Minister also spoke before the President and pleaded for the review of the constitution. According to the Prime Minister, while the constitution had stood the test of time, five decades after its adoption India was faced with a new situation. Apart from the acutely felt need for stability both at the centre and in the states, people were impatient for faster socio-economic development and the country is also faced with a pressing challenge to quickly remove regional and social imbalances by re-orienting the development process to benefit the poorest and the weakest. All this the Prime Minister felt warranted another look at the constitution. "Even in the mightiest fort one has to repair the parapet from time to time. One has to clean the moat and check the banisters......the same is true of our constitution."[17]

In spite of the Prime Minister strong plea for the review of the constitution, the President, while recounting the merit of the constitution, clearly and categorically stated: "Today when there is so much talk about revising the constitution or even writing a new constitution, we have to consider whether it is the constitution that has failed us or whether it is we who have failed the constitution."[18]

Demolishing the argument that instability of the government warranted constitutional change or a change over to a presidential form existing parliamentary form of government—a view shared by Prime Minister Vajpayee and Home Advani—the President maintained:

> "The form of government, the parliamentary democratic form, was chosen by the founding fathers after deep thought and debate. In the Constituent Assembly Dr. Ambedkar explained that the Drafting Committee, in choosing the parliamentary system for India, preferred more responsibility to more stability, a system under which the Government will be on the anvil every day. ...Our recent experience of instability system in favour of the Presidential or any other system."[19]

And finally the President also gave a same advice saying:

> "Whatever we may do, and we have a right to bring about necessary changes in the political and economic system, we should ensure that the basic philosophy behind the constitution and fundamental socio-economic soul of the constitution remain sacrosanct. We should not throw out the baby with bath water and like the tragic

character Othello in Shakespeare laments "like the base Indian, threw a pearl away—Richer than all his tribe."[20]

Efforts to Cover-up the Controversy

The President speech triggered off a controversy as the two Heads of the State were now openly in conflict with each other on an important issue on the agenda of the government. The Senior BJP leaders, therefore, swung into action to control the situation.

Ram Jethmalani, the then Law Minister tried to play down the "unseemly controversy" by asserting that there were no difference of opinion between the Prime Minister and the President on the question of review of the constitution. He maintained that "my reading of the President's speech is that he has approved of the process of keeping the constitution under review and making changes where necessary."[21]

Defending the governments stand on the issue, he pointed out three grounds for overhauling parts of the constitution: First, an altogether different situation that envisaged at the time of framing of the constitution; Second, if a section of the constitution was being interpreted or misused for public mischief; in the very first year, the constitution had to be amended to give effect to agrarian reforms. Third, if part of the philosophy of the constitution has been abandoned viz. the so-called socialism.[22]

The Union Home Minister L. K. Advani while speaking after inaugurating an exhibition, "We, the People of India" at the National Archives on 28 January 2000 be said:

> "We were given a mandate to rule. It is not related to the numbers in Parliament. It is a proper way that the commitment given by the NDA to the people is honoured. We had said that the period of 50 years of independent rule under the present constitution was an appropriate occasion to look at the constitution."[23]

Describing the review as a 'periodic health check-up' and referring to the Prime Minister's speech at the Central Hall of Parliament, Advani said:

> "Prime Minister merely re-affirmed what was said by the Government through the President's address to the joint session of Parliament after the Vajpayee Government came back to power....The intention is not to create a new constitution. We do not want create a new constitution. There is no question of altering the essential features and principles of the constitution."[24]

Defending the government's ground for an overall and integrated review of the constitution, Sushma Swaraj, a prominent BJP leader said that there were many questions like the eligibility of a person of foreign origin from contesting for the highest posts like that of Prime Minister and possible abuse of Article 356, which the fathers of the constitution had never anticipated. "Let us have a concrete answers to such questions."[25]

Finally, the government found out a way to cover-up in some way the aforesaid controversy. It utilized the opportunity of President's address to Parliament to defend its decision to set-up a commission to review he constitution. Reading from the text authored by the government the President said:

> "While keeping the basic structure and salient feature of the constitution inviolate, it has, however, become necessary to examine the experience of the past 50 years to better achieve the ideas enshrined in the constitution."[26]

In the same speech, the President also maintain that the constitution had served the people well and it has been a reliable guarantor of parliamentary democracy, secularism and fundamental rights. It has also inspired the spread of democratic consciousness in our society, empowering Dalits, Adivasis, backward classes and women and making our system of governance more participative and progressive.[27]

Finally, the government sought to allay fears about its move by declaring through the President that the reçommendations of the review panel would be presented before the Parliament, the final authority to decide on any changes.[28]

Constitutional Review Commission (CRC) Constituted

The controversy raised by the President did not deter the BJP from going for a review of the constitution. It did however constrain it to show a bold intent for a radical change of the constitution. The Government announced the formation of an 11-Member Constitutional Review Commission consisting of:

1. M. N. Venkatchalaih (A former SC Judge), Chairman
2. B. P. Jeeva Reddy (A Former SC Judge), Member
3. Justice R.S. Sarkaria, Member
4. Soli Sorabji (Attorney-General), Member
5. K. Parasaran (A former Attorney-General), Member
6. P. A. Sangma (A former L.S. Speaker), Member
7. Subhash Kashyap (A former L.S. S.G.), Member
8. Abid Hussain (A former Ambassador), Member
9. C. R. Irani, Editor-in-Chief, The Statesman, Member
10. Sumitra Kulkarni, Social Activist, Member
11. K. Punniah (A former Judge, APHC), Member

Nevertheless on account of the growing opposition to the idea of a review of the constitution, the government was compelled to keep the terms of reference of the CRC innocuous and confined to a singe point viz.: "to examine in the light of the experience of 50 years as to how best the constitution can respond to the changing needs of efficient, smooth and effective system of governance, socio-economic development of India within the frame work of parliamentary democracy and the recommend changes if any, that are required in the constitution without interfering with its basic structure."[29]

The term of reference of the CRC allayed to a great extent the general apprehension about the intention of the BJP which had evoked lot of criticism. It has now come to light that the terms of reference of the CRC were tailored in accordance with the views of the Chairman. While denying the fact that he had put some pre-conditions for accepting the responsibility Justice Venkatchaliah did openly confess:

> "It is not correct to say I have stipulated any conditions. However, I had indicated that the commission's terms of reference should be such that the basic features of the constitution and the parliamentary system of government are not put into debate."[30]

Further he made it amply clear that it was not for the commission to bring about changes in the constitution. "It is only the people's representatives that can do it. The Commission's work is essentially an academic exercise to collect the views of the civil society with the political society."[31]

Finally, commenting on the job of the CRC he stated:

"The exercise, as I see it, is essentially one to review how far the constitutional aspirations of the people of India have been realised and fulfilled...There is a vast array of issues that may need to be looked into, such as the election system, administration of justice, economic development and social opportunity, environmental safeguards, sustainable development, centre-state relations control of financial profligacy and fiscal policies, national integrity and security, the system for control of enormous corruption, etc."[32]

Apprehensions about the Review

The BJP's determined effort for a constitutional review had generated three-fold apprehensions. The first was that the BJP was trying to perpetuate itself in power. The past experience further tended to accentuate this kind of apprehension. During emergency, Indira Gandhi had also made similar venture. BJP's repeated emphasis on the concern for, stability of the government was therefore rightly considered by many as a pretext to remain entrenched in power.

The second apprehension was that in the name of constitutional review the BJP would replace the parliamentary form of government by a presidential one. Here also there was a parallelism between the BJP's move and Indira Gandhi's efforts during emergency. The close associate of Indira Gandhi during the emergency had launched a massive campaign for a Presidential form of government for the sake of stability. In the present situation the top leaders of the BJP and the RSS including Prime Minister Atal Behari Vajpayee and Home Minister L. K. Advani favoured the Presidential form of government. Precisely for that reason the government first wanted the former President Venkataraman to lead the CRC for his well known predilections and advocacy of the Presidential system. As early as in 1967 Venkataraman had come out with the suggestion to switch over to the Presidential system. Therefore, the move to appoint him as chairman of the CRC was vehemently opposed from several quarter and as a result it was dropped.

But the third apprehension which was of a more serious nature emanated from the notion of BJP being a fundamental party. Reacting to the proposal for a review, a journalist wrote: *"This is typical of all fascist and communist outfits which pretend that the policies were all wrong since they were formulated by anti-national people groups. Now the patriots are in charge, all the mistakes will be set right."*[33] A reputed political leader pointed out: *'There is a legitimate in the minds of many democrats that under the cover of reviewing the entire constitution, which according to various constitutional experts has stood the test of time efforts will be made to destroy the basic philosophy of the Constitution."*[34]

Thus there was a genuine fear in several quarters that BJP under the pretext of this review will introduce change in the vital aspects of the constitution to make it suit its ideology. The utterances of the BJP leaders and RSS men sustained this fear. K.S. Sudarshan who is now the RSS chief had highlighted the demerits of the constitution in an interview:

> "The present Constitution is but an extension of the Government of India Act. 1935, enacted by the British to serve their imperialistic objectives. Some chapters, drawing from other Constitutions, have been added, making it the biggest written Constitution. But it has still needed 80 amendments in 50 years.
>
> The gray areas that need a through review are: The Federal structure, devolution of powers to the lower units, democracy at the grassroots, the method of representation where a majority of popular votes props up governments, unstable government, frequent elections, growing money and muscle power, unsbashed political horsetrading, irresponsible and unresponsive bureaucracy.

The review commission will examine how far the Westminster type of parliamentary democracy has been beneficial to us, and whether it needs changes."[35]

Earlier, in an issue of the Organiser, the RSS mouthpiece, it was maintained that the constitutional review should reflect Indian ethos, underlining the fact that we are "one people, one nation, one culture."[36]

Hence, the general apprehension of the review was that the BJP will try to destroy the cultural plurality of the nation and also the parliamentary democracy, which is considered as a segment of the basic structure of the constitution.

Criticisms: Political Parties, Press and Public

Supporting the view of the President the leader of opposition in the Kerala Assembly and a member of the Congress Working Committee criticised the BJP for its attempt of tampering with the Constitution.[37] The AIADMK condemned it as a *calculated move of the Prime Minister to turn the constitution on its head.*[38] The CPI and the CPI-M endorsed the President's view of the futility of the exercise. A CPI-M leader, Sitaram Yechury has stated: *"The BJP is trying to undermine the secular foundations of the constitution. They have a theocratic Hindu Rashtra in mind, and the RSS in fact, feets that the present constitution is un-Hindu."*[39]

A former Chief Justice of India A. M. Ahmadi expressed his doubts saying:

> "In the life of a country's constitution, 50 years is not sufficiently long to call for its replacement. If the idea is to review the constitution in its entirety, I am afraid it is premature. But if the objective is to review certain gray areas only that may be different."[40]

Academicians also opposed the move of constitutional review. It was maintained: "In normal circumstances, a review does not really call for such a hue and cry. But in this case, it is not in the national interest—it is motivated by sectional party interest."[41] According to C. P. Bhambhari—

> "It is trap being laid by the BJP and they will be successful in delegitimising the constitution and raising in the minds of the people doubts about it. They will use TV/radio—the government media—and politically divide the country on the issue of the constitution."[42]

An eminent sociologist, T. K. Oommen was still more vehement and direct in his following criticism:

> "The BJP's motive is to convince the people that cultural nationalism will be more effective than the cultural pluralism endorsed by the constitution. Through the review, they can communicate to the masses that there is an alternative way of building the nation."[43]

And finally, Upendra Baxi wrote a full length article tearing to pieces all arguments of the RSS-BJP combine for constitutional review any aptly termed the exercise as *"Kar Seva of the Indian Constitution."*[44]

Concluding Observations

Review of a Constitution *per se* is not objectionable. At the bicentennial of the American Constitution, a committee went into the American constitutional system and expressed its views. Some of the papers are published in *Reforming American Government* by Donald L. Robinson. In the case of the Indian constitution, this is not the first attempt for review. Several attempts have been made in the past. The first such exercise resulted in the ninth amendment to the Constitution which bars judicial review of entries in it. In 1954, a sub-committee of the Congress Working Committee produced such an anti-judiciary report that Nehru thought it better to suppress it. Decision in the 'Golaknath' case in 1967, paved the way for another review. Nath Pai's bill led to twenty-fourth amendment declaring that Parliament could amend the constitution by way of addition, variation or repeats which culminated in the apex court's 'basic structure' doctrine in the Kesvanand Bharati case. In 1976 Swaran Singh Committee undertook another exercise which culminated in the 42nd amendment. This was undone by the Janata Party Government through 43rd and 44th amendments. In 1980 Justice R. S. Sarkaria was asked to review with the focus on centre-state relations.

In all these cases except Mrs. Gandhi's exercise during emergency there was hardly any adverse reaction. On the contrary an eminent jurist and a fiery defender of civil liberty in the country has rightly maintain that it is eminently in the public interest and in the Government's own interest that constitutional amendments should be the subject matter of an 'open public debate and not of a whispering campaign'.[45] In fact, in a liberal democratic set-up, the constitution remains under constant review by the press, public, political parties, parliament, courts and media and the government of the day should be watchful and honest enough to take cue from such review for appropriate constitutional amendments in public interest.

The BJP's exercise is totally devoid of this spirit. Besides, it has been prompted by selfish interest of the party and its command organisation, the RSS. There is a general feeling that the constitutional changes are favoured for removing obstacles to implementing the hidden agenda. It is pertinent to note in this connection that although the government under the pressure of public criticisms has conceded in the terms of reference of the CRC to treat parliamentary system as part of the basic structure, the RSS Chief, K.S. Sudarshan, still maintained that "the review commission will examine how far the Westminister type of parliamentary democracy has been beneficial to us, and whether it needs changes."[46]

The BJP's logic of the review is foolhardy: 'To say that is doing it in pursuance of its pledge to the electorate at the time of the Lok Sabha election in 1999 which voted it to power' lacks conviction. The pledge in the election manifesto does not convincingly give the party a mandate to interfere with the constitution. Few of the country's voters are aware of the NDA's manifesto and voted because of it. Moreover, the various grounds mentioned by the BJP for a review of the constitution are far from satisfactory.

Let us take for instance its stability argument. The BJP should know that stability of government is not the virtue of democracy. The virtue of parliamentary democracy is accountability, not stability. The framers of the Indian constitution preferred responsibility to stability which could slip into authoritarian exercise of power. Indira Gandhi used the pretext of stability for authoritarian exercise of power and now the BJP is doing the same.

The argument that stability is essential as the country can hardly afford the waste of time, energy and above all money involved in frequent elections may appeal to a common man but not to an enlightened citizen who understands the value of democracy. One should not forget that democracy is a precious thing and the country should remain prepared to pay any price to preserve its existence and purity. The government is oblivious of, and insensitive to, the gigantic waste and reckless misuse of public money by governmental machinery itself but it is questioning the expenses on election. Election expenses should not be treated as waste in a truly democratic system.

The BJP's means for attaining stability by re-fixing the term of the Lok Sabha will do more harm than good to the spirit of our constitution. If provisions are made for the Lok Sabha to complete its term of five years without any danger of its being dissolved prior to that, then what will happen if a government is voiced out in the hours and no alternative government is formed? This will pave way for continuance of a government in power even after having lost the confidence of the house. Moreover, when members of Parliament are assured of their full five-years tenure, they will be risk-free to change their allegiance for the sake of even peripheral benefit and this will in fact accentuate the instability of the government rather than ensure stability. Therefore any attempt to interfere with the well-established principles and procedures of parliamentary democracy may be counterproductive.

Further, the BJP's plea for constructive vote of confidence has no relevance to the review of the constitution. The constructive vote of no-confidence is a German innovation, inscribed in that country's Basic Law. If adopted here, the Lok Sabha may express its lack of confidence in the incumbent Prime Minister by electing his successor with the majority of its members. It seeks to reduce political instability, by requiring the House not to be guided by purely negative or cavalier moves. A change to this effects does not necessitate a review of the constitution or its amendment, not even a simple legislative measure. It could be brought about by revising the rules of procedure of the Lok Sabha as was done when the concept of confidence motion was introduced, subjecting the Government or the Prime Minister to a test of strength.

Another argument which the protagonists of the party advance to justify the review is that the conditions attaining at the time of framing of the constitution more than half a century ago have changed and, therefore, a fresh look at the constitution is needed. This argument cuts no ground. The constitution during this period has been amended 80 times to suit the changing time and need of the country. The constitution itself has some amount of ingrained adaptability as well as procedural provisions to refurbish its relevance and workability.

The BJP's constitutional review exercise suffers from many other shortcomings. The government has not taken the parliament into confidence on the question. The decision to constitute a CRC is not the result of parliamentary deliberations and consensus. To propose a review of the constitution without even a discussion in Parliament about the desirability of such an exercise is automatically to rob the entire undertaking of legitimacy.

Again, in appointing a panel for the review the government did not think it proper to include in it the members of Parliament. This will naturally make the eventual findings of the commission democratically a suspect. Former Prime Minister V. P. Singh was right when he called upon the Vajpayee Government to constitute a parliamentary committee instead of a commission for the proposed review of the constitution.[47]

This is not to undermine the stature of the members of the CRC in any way. The panel does comprise eminent and honourable persons. But the democratic fabric of the polity is severely compromised if such a group is seen to be a collection of wise men who do not represent the popular will. On the other hand, "the panel has individuals who are currently associated with certain political outfits or have been part of earlier Governmental dispensation. This dilutes the all important criterion of impartiality" of the commission.[48]

The whole exercise is bound to be futile. It is futile because the CRC can only make recommendations and those recommendations can be incorporated in the constitution only through amendments. The present government is not is a position to do so. It does not have the requisite majority either in the Lok Sabha or in the Rajya Sabha for amending the constitution.

Besides, it is doubtful whether all the partners of the coalition government will ultimately support the BJP on such an important issue of amendment of the constitution. Their ideological differences are most likely to be roadblock to any attempt for a radical change.

Moreover, keeping in mind the fate of the coalition governments, it just possible that by the time the CRC submits its recommendations, the NDA may not be in the ruling position.

It is also meaningless because the CRC is not supposed to recommend anything against the 'basic structure' of the constitution including the change of parliamentary form which the BJP-RSS combine so much desired. The open opposition of the President and public fury have drastically curtailed the options of the CRC in making recommendations for constitutional changes.

Nobody is under illusion to expect anything worthwhile and remarkable from this exercise. On the contrary the functioning of the CRC for more than a year now provide tangible evidence to its disappointing performance. By confining itself merely to ten issues, the CRC has drastically narrowed down nay nullified the stated purpose of the review. Secondly, the commission has not allowed transparency in its functioning. It allows only certain things to reach the people for fruitful reaction and interaction. The commission has opinion of the people, but it has no mechanism for methodically obtaining opinions and comments.

Moreover, whatever information is available regarding the thinking and suggestions of the CRC, has only created adverse reaction not only among the people in general but also of the President of India. For instance, citing the method of indirect election as propounded by the Mahatma Gandhi the CRC too has floated this suggestion contained in a consultation paper circulated by it, presumably to show respect to the father of the nation which the Constituent Assembly had failed to do. But the CRC has forgotten that Gandhi's context of indirect election was quite different. The system of indirect election can hardly be in consonance with the parliamentary democracy. Not unnaturally, the President of India, in his address to the nation on the eve of the Republic Day on 25 January 2001 contemptuously disapproved this suggestion which, according to him, reflected the shades of political ideas of the father of military rule in Pakistan, Field Marshall Ayub Khan.

The President further observed that the founding father had the wisdom and foresight not to over-emphasize the importance of stability and uniformity of the political system and consciously rejected the system of restricted franchise and indirect elections embodied in the Government of India Act of 1935. The President reminded: "It (indirect election) requires a profound faith in the wisdom of the common man and woman in India. Today it is necessary to look back to this faith when we hear voices pleading for a system of indirect elections."[49]

Above all, the working of the Election Panel of the CRC has all the more dismayed people. The fact which has come to light is indeed shocking. And finally, to maintain that the review of the constitution will facilitate the process of the realizing the dreams of the framers of the constitution especially in the context of social justice has no substance in it. The constitution has not been a hindrance to this. For failure of the system to attain the goals set by the founding fathers, there is need to improve the quality of politics and public life and inculcate a sense of moral responsibility among the people in general and those in power in particular.

References

1. Cited in Text of the Indian President Speech, *Mainstream* (New Delhi), 12 February 2000, p. 9.
2. *Ibid.*, p. 10.
3. *Ibid.*
4. *Ibid.*
5. Cited in N.A. Palkhivala, *We the People: Indira—The Largest Democracy* (Bombay, 1984), p. 41.
6. *Mainstream,* 12 February 2000, p. 10.
7. *Ibid.*
8. Palkhivala, n. 5, p. 4.
9. *Hindustan Times* (New Delhi), 23 February 2000.
10. Durga Das Basu, *Introduction to the Constitution of India* (New Delhi, 1999), p. 153.
11. *Times of India* (New Delhi), 26 March, 1998.
12. NDA's Election Manifesto (1999).
13. *Times of India,* 26 October 1999.
14. Dev Dutta, 'BJP and the Review of the Constitution", *Young Indian* (New Delhi), 12 February 2000, p. 6.
15. *Hindustan Times,* 26 January 2000.
16. *Ibid.*
17. *The Hindu* (New Delhi), 28 January 2000.
18. *Ibid.*

19. *Text of the President's Speech,* n. 1, pp. 9-11.
20. *Ibid.*
21. *The Hindu* 29 January 2000.
22. *Ibid.*
23. *Ibid.*
24. *Ibid.*
25. *Hindustan Times,* 31 January 2000.
26. *Ibid.*, 23 February 2000.
27. *Ibid.*
28. *Ibid.*
29. *Times of India,* 15 February 2000.
30. Interview of M. N. Venkatachaliah by Akshaya Mukul, *Hindustan Times,* 6 February 2000.
31. *Ibid.*
32. *Ibid.*
33. Amulya Ganguli, "Fiddling with the System", *Ibid.*, 6 February 2000.
34. *Times of India,* 11 February 2000.
35. K. S. Sudarshan's Interview by Rajesh Ramachandran, *Ibid.*, 20 February 2000.
36. *Organiser* (New Delhi), 6 February 2000.
37. *The Hindustan Times,* 28 January 2000.
38. *The Hindu,* 29 January 2000.
39. *Economic Times* (New Delhi), 6 February 2000.
40. *Hindustan Times,* 28 January 2000.
41. Dipankar Gupta, *Economic Times,* 6 February 2000.
42. *Ibid.*
43. *Ibid.*
44. Upendra Baxi, 'Kar Seva of the Indian Constitution? Reflection on Proposals for Review of the Constitutions". *Economic and Political Weekly,* 11 March 2000.
45. Palkhivala, n. 5.
46. K. S. Sudarshan's Interview by Rajesh Ramchandran, *Hindustan Times,* 20 February 2000.
47. *Ibid.*, 31 January 2000.
48. Editorial, *Times of India,* 15th February 2000.
49. *Hindustan Times,* 29 January 2001.

6

Uniform Civil Code: A Prelude to Good Governance

S. K. Chaturvedi

Hon'ble Supreme Court of India while delivering a judgment in the case of Christian priest John Vallamattom (Kerala) on 27-7-2003 opined that "it is a matter of regret that Article 44 of the constitution has not been given effect to. Parliament is still to step in for forming a civil code in the country. A common civil code will help the cause of national integration by removing the contradictions based on ideology"[1] This view of the apex court has once again opened the debate in connection with section 44 of the constitution which envisage that "the state shall endeavour to secure for the citizens a uniform civil code throughout the territory of India". This is not for the first time that the judiciary has made a *fervent* appeal to the national legislature but earlier too while pronouncing judgment against Polygamy (Narasu Appa Mali V/s. State of Bombay (1952), Srinivas Aiyar V/s. Saraswathi Ammal (1952), Ram Prasad. V/s. State of U.P. (1957), Itwari V/s. Asghari (1960), Shahulamedu V/s. Zubaida Beevi (1970), B Chandra Manil Kyamma V/s. B Sudershan (1989).

In the cases relating to property, succession, divorce, maintenance and adoption different High Courts and apex court made such appeal. But the political and social leadership have failed to rise to the occasion and ensure an egalitarian social structure striving for social justice, secular polity, integrity and unity of the nation, dignity of individual, stability to the polity and social change while converting a heterogeneous society into a homogeneous one and saving the nation from further division on religious and gender lines. An effort is being made in this paper to ponder over the issue.

At the very outset, it would be relevant to understand the meaning of twin terms 'civil' and 'code'. The dictionary meaning of world 'civil' connotes a human society wherein people are living together with certain rights and performing some duties and 'code' means a system of rules and principles that has been accepted by the society or a class or group of people' thus civil code strives for keeping a human society together with the help of a system of rule or principle based on consciousness. It is in this perspective that the framers of Indian Constitution aspired for a *uniform* civil code, to keep the plural social structure together and perhaps the plurality of the polity and socio, political environment prevailing at the time of independence that they kept this aspiration in the chapter of the 'Directive Principle of state Policies', to be attained by the state in due course of time. Otherwise the same could have been a part of preamble or incorporated in the chapter of the Fundamental Rights. It may not be out of place to mention here that in present times in none of the country the uniform civil code is an issue. Than why it is in our country? While seeking an answer to this question we may have to peep in the hoary past and the existing constitutional provisions in this regard. And looking into efforts made by the state in the context, contribution of the judiciary to carry out the objective. Politicians and legislature's apathy in the context and finding out whether such a code is necessary for 'good governance' and if so what steps are desirable to be taken in this perspective.

Historical Backdrop

Ancient Hindu scriptures speak that since it was divinely in spired, law was uniform in Hindu society. The sages expounded laws on the principles rooted in the vedas. Hindu laws were largely secular in character as evident from the Arthasastra of Kautilya. Positive law was differentiated from the religious lore. These law preached ethics, morality and governed social life of the times. Religion was considered to be performance of duties. The relationship between the king and his subject was based on rule of law. In Hindu polity king was not considered divine in that spirit as was considered in Greek, Chinese, Egyptian and European civilizations. In Rigveda the king is referred to as 'Ardha-divine'. King Parikshit has been described in Atharva-veda as god amongst men and not an incarnation of god. Hence Hindu system of law though was divine but was based on social customs and traditions (Altaker) being reviewed by the sages from time to time. In other words, society was above the state and religion, law was an integral part of religion and religion was determinant of rights and duties.

By the end of eleventh century, Muslims became a political reality in Indian system resulting into disorganization of Hindu society and paving the path of induction of Muslim personal law *i.e,.* social customs and traditions through which Islamic society was being regulated and governed. The invaders did not accept Hindu law nor they interfered in them resulting into existence of Hindu and Mohammadan personal law during the entire medieval age of India's history. However in the case of criminal laws largely uniformity in respect of both communities were maintained.

Britishers though did not interfere with laws governing Hindu and Muslim communities but codified certain laws applicable in common to both the communities. They realized that general legislation is essential for the unity of the country. Hence, they enacted new laws to replace and reform the traditional Hindu or Muslim laws so as to ensure social progress, societal control and change. The appointment of different law commissions* is a testimony to the fact that the Britisher's endeavour was to achieve the object of uniform legislations applicable alike to all the people irrespective to their religious belief. As such, Indian Penal Code, Cr. P.C. (1898), Caste Disability Removal Act, (1850) Indian contract Act. 1872, succession Act 1865, child marriage Act 1928. code of civil procedure, 1859 were enacted.

From the above resume it is evident that the uniform personal law which was prevailing in Hindu Society in ancient times was not acceptable to the invaders and as such they promulgated their own personal laws. Hence on the eve of independence two sets of personal laws were in prevalence putting hurdles before the unity and integrity of the nation. Considering the fact, the founding fathers thought about a uniform civil code *i.e,*. in the case of marriage, succession, divorce etc there should be uniform law for all the communities so as to achieve the goals of protection of human right of the individual, unity and integrity of nation, social justice and as such chartering the path of progress and development so as to converting the heterogeneous Indian society into a homogeneous entity while saving the country from further fractionalization on religious or caste lines. Article 44 of the constitution has been enacted with the spirit that state need to promote congenial environment so that our democracy grows on healthy grounds.

However, in constituent Assembly members of minority community particularly Mohammedans opposed the proposal on the grounds that:

(a) Personal law is a comprehensive code of life and has its origin in divine revelation and therefore immutable. Muslim laws relating to marriage, divorce and inheritance have been handed down by the prophet and are in the sense divine, and therefore unquestionably obeyed. Mohd. Isamil, Pocker Bahadur, Mehboob Ali beg, Naziruddin Ahmed, Hussain Imam as members of constituent Assembly vehemently opposed the provision.

It is worthwhile to note that members of all other minority communities *i.e,*. Christian, Parsi, Sikh, Buddhist and Jain supported the very idea of uniform civil code.

The proposal of uniform civil code is being opposed by the orthodox Muslims whereas was being supported by the progressive and secular Muslims. The secularists like Hamid Dalvi felt that uniform civil code is necessary to free the Muslim women from male slavery. He was in favour of registration of marriages, legally banning purdah and making family planning compulsory. They feel that Muslims in the country should not be allowed to remain backward. They must progress and for this purpose if Muslims personal law is to be changed it must be changed. Obviously, on the issue of uniform civil code, whereas the major minority community stood as divided house rest of the minority communities had no objection. The jurists, legal luminaries and press all were in favour of enactment of such a code. For instance-Justice P.V. Gajendra Gadkar was of opinion that the Muslim personal law is not in tune with the democratic traditions of country and therefore must be changed. It would be in the interest of development of *secularism* in India to have a uniform civil code. In the same vain Justice Hedge maintained that the government should not hesitate to enact a uniform civil code even on the face of opposition, from some quarters while guaranteeing *social justice* to all. V.K. Krishna Iyyar, another legal luminary viewed that civil code is necessary from the angle of national integration. He further stated that one country, one nationality, one citizenship and one legal system is axiomatic and we can not think in terms of personal laws that vary with communities, religion and sects.

Hon'ble Supreme Court and High Courts while pronouncing their judgment in the cases relating to polygamy, succession, divorce and maintenance fervently appealed to the national legislature to make efforts for realizing the directive of having a uniform civil code. For instance in the Narasu *Appa Mali V/s. State of Bombay* case relating to Polygamy Mr. Justice M. C. Chagla opined that there should not be any legal discrimination between Muslim and Hindu communities on the basis of religion. Justice P. V. Gajendra Gadkar while delivering his judgment in the same case opined that state should put efforts in securing a uniform civil code throughout the territory in India. In another case of *Srinivasa Aiyar V/s. Saraswathi Ammal (1952)* Madras High Court pronounced that state was empowered to regulate religious practices through appropriate legislation whenever it was in the interest of social welfare and intended for social reforms. In the cases of Ram Prasad V/s. state of U.P. (1957), Itwari V/s. Asghari (1960), Sahula Meedau V/s. Zubaida Beevi (1970) and B Chandra Manil Kyamma V/s. B Sudershan (1989). Hindu and Islamic personal laws were kept aside by the Hon'ble Court. The same attitude was adopted by the court in the matters of succession. In the cases of Smt. Gurdial Kaur V/s. Mangal Singh (1968), Md. Abu Zafar V/s. Israr Ahmed (1971) etc. The pronouncements made by the courts encouraged the environment of uniform legislation for all communities. The courts in India have sought to establish a secular polity founded on social justice irrespective of the tenets of religion. It has always tried to implement section 44 of the constitution in words and spirit irrespective of religious emotions of the people as evident from the decision pronounced by it in the famous cases (Narasu Appa Mali, Shahbano Begum, Saira Banu, J. V. Safia) cited above.

The courts view has been that personal law should be curtailed if it comes in conflict with the general law of the land designed to promote the welfare of the community at large. Contrary to this the legislature has failed considerably in promoting the philosophy enshrined in Article 44 of the constitution that " the state shall endeavour to secure for the citizens a uniform civil code through out the territory of India". Whatever little it has done is in the context of majority Hindu community. Based on the Rau Committee (1941) report it has passed Hindu code bill, Hindu marriage Act. (1955) succession Act (1956), Hindu minority Act (1955) and Hindu adoption bill (1956). In the case of minority community it could enact controversial Muslim women (Protection of Rights and Divorce) Act 1956 resulting into eclipsing of the prospect of a uniform civil code. It may be relevant to note here that it is the- women population of India which is most effected in the absence of such a code on the count of marriage, divorce and adoption, institution of joint family, succession etc. As a result of which the basic values of equality, social justice, rule of law, are jeopardized and in absence of which the very objectives of national unity, integrity and the dignity of individual can not be achieved, that are essential for the building of a nation, vibrant democratic structure and responsive good governance. A nation perhaps can not afford that 11.67 percent of the people of minority community queer the path of progress and development and dignity of 82.41 percent of its population, political stability, perpetual peace and objective of good governance. It may not be out of place to mention here that the objective of good governance can only be achieved if Human Rights of the people are protected and rule of law is maintained. Needless to mention that in absence of universal civil code, rights of women and infants are trampled. On the name of religion, they are the ultimate sufferers. The value of secularism becomes a causality. One of the protagonists of minority community, Tahir Mehmood has rightly suggested that if the goal of secularism is to be achieved religion based personal law need to be amended. On the other hand, Muslim clergy leader like Banatwala is of opinion that peace may be endangered if any law infringing Muslim personal law is enacted. In such a situation it seems desirable on the part of policy planner to educate the members of minority community in favour of the universal civil code and for the purpose mass media, educational institutions, local self institutions need to be taken into confidence. One must not forget that ignorance is the greatest hurdle in the way of enactment of such law. Political will on the part of political leadership is also desirous. Perhaps, afraid of losing minority vote that the leadership is shaky in taking bold decisions. But one should not forget that in pre-independence days four laws effecting Islamic way of life *i.e,*. marriage, wakf, shariat and dissolution of marriage were enacted and were accepted by the minority community. It also accepted six laws relating to succession, contract, evidences alongwith CrPC, IPC and CPC during the said period. If the community could accept all these laws then why it will not agree to the universal civil code? Only political courage on the part of legislature is required. Further a committee of Jurists may be appointed with the purpose to frame a code in respect of marriage, talaq, inheritance, adoption, maintenance and succession etc. The committee may keeping best of the personal laws of majority and minority communities after extracting consciousness on common acceptable areas may be implemented. The areas where difference of opinion exist may be left for the time being. However, efforts may continued to be made in the direction. It need to be remembered that 'state is to remove barriers towards attaining rule of law' and non- existence of a universal code of law in the greatest hurdle in the way of rule of law. In last half a century the Indian judiciary has striven hard to establish a secular polity founded on social justice but the political leadership has failed to rise to the cause. Since fundamentalists of the minority community want to retain their hold on the community they deliver threatening statements against peace and unity of the country whenever any effort in the direction is made. There is a need of taking people into confidence, who are anchor sheet of a democratic system and are striving for a peaceful, dignified, and egalitarian life and aspire for adjusting the country to changing needs, promotion of national unity, maintenance of uniformity of law and equality of persons including equality of sex and ameliorate the condition of women and down trodden sections of society and for that reason a uniform civil code is the primary requirement.

References

1. *The Hindu*, Delhi, July 24, 2003.
2. *Oxford Advanced Learner's Dictionary*, Oxford, 1974, pp. 181-184.

*. In 1833, 1853, 1861, 1870
Hastings effort, 1772
Succession Act, 1865
Child marriage Restrain Act, 1928
IPC-1861, Cr. PC., 1898
CPC, 1859
Indian Contract Act, 1872
Evidence Act, 1872
Succession 1865

7

Discourse on Good Governance: Some Reflections on Indian Experience

Madhurendra Kumar

Quest for excellence in human life has been the perennial concern of political discourse in all the ages. Since the very inception of human civilization and organized living, one of the priorities of governments has been to ensure a better living standard for its people. The history of political philosophy, both oriental and occidental is replete with numerous endeavours that aimed at promoting good life to the people. So the notion of Good Governance cannot be said to be recent discourse, rather it is as old as human civilization.

Even in the age of 'monarchy and legitimized ascriptive inequality' there have been debates to determine the indicators of good governance. Kautilya in his Arthasastra 'looks upon the king as servant of the state who has no personal likes, rather, it would be the likes of servants that would be followed by him'.[1] He merges his individuality with public duties. As described by K.P. Jaiswal, 'king was the 'Constitutional Slave'.[2] He acts in concert with the seven organs of the state and values their opinion. In all his acts, the primary concern was the welfare of the people and in discharging his duties, he is expected to adhere to the tradition of 'Swadharma'. His swadharma guides him to see that no person transgresses the categories and canons of swadharma of others'. According to Kautilya, a the king must ensure that social disorganization does not set in. He has laid down in his 'Arthasastra' a comprehensive plan to ensure good governance through a large and complex administrative mechanism and enunciated principles of public finance. The king in his schematic arrangement of governance was to look after the people and had to be solicitous for the welfare of the children, the aged, the orphans, the afflicted and other people who are the victims of calamities.[3] Kautilya writes- "In their happiness, in their welfare whatever pleases him (personally) he shall not consider as good but whatever makes his subjects happy he shall consider good." "The Santiparva" also lays down postulates, precepts, maxims and norms of temporal and social pyramidal hierarchical organization, which aims at preventing disruption, disorder in the social structure. A code of conduct laid down for the king refers to formulation of 'mantracinta' *i.e,*. policies for the promotion and fostering of the happiness of the people.[4] Guidelines for good governance are exclusively mentioned in "The Santiparava". 'The foundation of good governance is Dharma. The king and the ministers and state employees who have taken the oath of their offices to uphold 'dharma' and to act in accordance with the 'common Good' must not act unjustly or unethically so as to secure their private good through selfishness. If they don't behave appropriately, they all will surely go to hell along with destroying the moral basis of governance." Even in Bhagwatgeeta, the objective of governance is to protect and sustain the common good.[5] In fact, the concern of governance is wider in the tradition of ancient Indian thought than the western notion of common good. It is the notion of 'Dharma' that regulates public affairs during ancient times. It includes in its domain not only human beings but all the beings in the creation.[6]

Similarly, in western tradition of political thinking also we find enough discourse pertaining to governance for the common good. Plato, the famous Greek Political thinker, in his 'Republic', express his concern to make the life of citizens good and virtuous.[7] Aristotle's state exists for the sake of good life. He says "city is best governed which has the greatest opportunity of obtaining happiness".[8] Even for Thomas Aquinas the promotion of the common good was always the main concern of the government.[9] Similarly Lockes, Rousseau, Bentham and Mill have elaborately discussed the schemes and objectives of governance in their thoughts and have given adequate attention to provide safeguards to individual freedom and welfare. Thus, these accounts testify that the idea of good governance has its roots in the ancient times. Of course, nomenclature and semantics vary from time to time. Nevertheless the cardinal concern of all these enterprises has been to ascertain the welfare, peace and prosperity to the people through governance.

However, it became a buzzword for administrative reforms towards the end of the 20th century in view of the chronic laxity of the governments in the third world country to carry forward the goals of development to the grass root level. This idea perhaps sprang from the challenges of development in the third world countries where bureaucracy continues to demonstrate an almost 'trained incapacity, isolation from the people, excessive concern, misplaced faith in the capabilities of the administrations and inability to adapt to the changes.'[10] Politics became the means to power and Government–the manifestation of the quest for domination. Governance, administration and management lost relevance and were reduced to mere techniques of ruling over the people. Public offices became the place of self aggrandizements. While these countries are densely populated, they are most illiterate malnourished and least gender sensitive. Unemployment, distressingly large-scale poverty, disease and sufferings are the characteristics of the third world countries. This scenario persisting in the third world countries led Mahbub-ul Haq, the pioneer of the Human Development Centre in Pakistan to conclude that root cause of the failure of governments in the sphere of responsive efficient and effective government is due to crises of governance.[11]

Thus, it is clear that the concept of good governance derives its relevance in the context of mis-governance which includes 'non-feasance', and 'malfeasance', failure to prevent the swindling of public funds for private gains by the elected leaders as well as the bureaucrats. Misuse of power, fraud, chicanery and embezzlement of funds are systematically, perpetrated by the leaders of government and their minions: His Governance pervades in all segments of the polity in rampant degree.[12] In this context of mismanagement of Public administration, the concept of good governance acquired prominence in contemporary discourse of public administration.

Therefore, the aid donor countries laid the condition of structural changes, democratization and improvement of human rights records for providing assistance to developing countries in the 1980s and 1990s and insisted on ascertaining good governance.

The dominant discourse of Good Governance was promoted by the World Bank and other proponents of new liberal economic globalization as a means of effective management of economic resources.

As a concept, 'Good Governance' found expression for the first time in a World Bank document on Sub Saharan Africa. Good Governance, according to this document, stood for sound development management and it has four major aspects: (i) Public Sector Management (ii) Accountability (iii) Legal framework for development and (iv) Information and transparency. In this scheme accountability, rule of law, openness and transparency were emphasized.[13]

Thus, terms like governance and Good Governance found entry in development literature. Bad governance now came to be regarded as one of the root causes of underdevelopment and poor administration in different societies. The World Bank described governance as the manner in his power is exercised in the management of a country's economic and social resources for development. It noted that inspite of technical soundness, programmes and projects have not yielded desired outcomes. Rule enforcement is weak and red tapism often delays implementation of the developmental programmes. So, it led emphasis on economic, human and institutional development through governance. What was ignored in the World Bank's prescription is that Good Governance was not just the effective management of economic resources, it is about freedom, human rights, public accountability and peoples participation. Hence, Organization for Economic Cooperation and Development (OECD) linked legitimacy of the government, accountability of political and official segment of government viz. media, freedom, transparent decision, making accountability mechanisms, competence of governments to design policies and deliver goods and services, safeguards of human rights and rule of law, individual and group rights and security framework for economic and social activity and participation[14] etc. to the notion of Good Governance.

Even the international Monetary Fund acknowledged 'good governance is important for countries at all stages of development'.[15] So, it has long provided advice and technical assistance that has helped to foster good governance such as promoting public sector transparency and accountability. Traditionally the IMF' s main focus has been on encouraging countries to correct macroeconomic imbalances, reduce inflation and undertake key trade exchange and other market reforms needed to improve efficiency and support sustained economic growth. In its declaration 'partnership for sustainable global growth', the IMF interview committee on September 29, 1996 identified, 'promoting good governance in all its aspects including ensuring the rule of law, improving the efficiency and the public sector and tackling corruption as an essential element of framework within which economics can prosper.[16]

Besides these dimensions of Good Governance, new liberals propounded the concept of 'rolling back of the state' as a pre-condition for good governance. They argued that withdrawal of status should make room for voluntary sector, NGOs on one hand and free market force on the other. The role of NGOs in good governance is justified on the ground that it not only promotes popular participation in development rather it bridges the gap between local community and administration.[17]

In fact, the dominant discourse of good governance promoted by the World Bank, IMF, OECD and other proponents of neo-liberal economic globalization lays emphasis on effective management of economic resources. It is a techno-managerial approach that focuses on decentralization, transparency and report cards as ways to ensure macro economic management as proposed by the 'Bretton Woods Mandarins'. It tends to seek accountability from national governments for the economic and political conditions imposed on them. The main agenda behind the idea of good governance mooted by the multilateral and bilateral trade agencies like the World Bank, UNDP, OECD and ADB etc. was to ascertain the success of their projects. Their major thrust was on structural adjustment and economic reformd programmes consisting of liberalization, deregulation, privatization and state withdrawal from economic spheres.

What is ignored in such discourses is the fact that governance is a broader concept. It is about power relationship within and beyond institutions and is based on the notion of accountability and answerability. It provides the institutional means to rights and seeks justice through justice delivery system. It is the interface through which citizens mediate and interact with the state and seek accountability. Therefore a viable paradigm of good governance must address the issues of budget tracking, participation, monitoring, planning process, citizens charter, report cards, women's empowerment, public hearing, grievance redressal and public, interest litigations. This framework calls for people's empowerment to seek accountability and ask questions. So, the perspective on good governance should be informed by the perspective of people's empowerment, participation, public accountability and transparency, human rights and legitimacy based on the principles democracy.[18] On the basis of the above discussion, it may be said that Good governance is a dynamic concept demanding periodical review, rethinking and remodeling of the institutions of governance, enhancing accountability and transparency, so as to secure socio economic and political justice, liberty of thought, expression, belief, faith and equality of status and opportunity. In order to attain these objectives, the constitution of India directed the welfare of the people, equitable distribution of material resources to sub-serve the common good. These grandiose goals set by the constitution have been lost on the wayside and Good Governance in India has become a casualty by the 'vacuity of vision' 'absence of mission' and 'lack of leadership'. Consequently, India's quest for good governance became a casualty during the 55 years of independence as we failed to take measures to prevent the onslaught impact the institutional deterioration and decline of values in socio-political life.

The progressive decline, malfunctioning and corruption in the functioning of the executive, the entry of persons of doubtful integrity and even of criminal background in the political sphere, the established role of money and muscle power in the electoral process, the failure of the state legislature and the parliament to *inter alia*, effectively perform their mandated watchdog role over the functioning of the executive, the politicians, casteisiation, communalization and corruption of the services, the operation of criminal nexus with politicians, growing incidence of violence, of subversion and sabotage in various parts of the country, continuing serious failure of the public delivery system, erosion of integrity of public institution including universities and centres of excellence.[19]

This scenario of Indian political and administrative culture speaks volumes of the challenges before good governance in India. The experience of 55 years of Indian administrative system in the post independence India shows that the fore most challenge is that of institutional governance. The capacities of the institutions to deliver services efficiently and effectively have eroded over a period of time, so much so, that one is constrained to believe that the mechanism has broken down and institutional arrangements need to be revamped in order to the make public delivery system efficient because it would not only check the wastage of public expenditure. Rather it would enhance the efficiency of the system as well. Therefore, there is urgent need for reorienting the structure and functioning of public service delivery organization.[20]

Another formidable challenge before good governance in India is corruption. It is eating into the vitals of the system of governance. Financial discipline has evaporated many states. Political interference in the day to day affair has increased to alarming proportion. So much so that no room for integrity and autonomy is left for bureaucrats for independent and judicious decision. Instead of appointing impartial, judicious and upright bureaucrats, the political leadership often appoint persons of their choice so that they can subserve partisan and personal interest of the political bosses. As a result, lobbying for often posting continues unabated. Outstanding officers are overlooked and ministers preferred corrupt and in competent men. This tendency has led to a rise in political interference in the matters of transfers and postings to get plum postings. Minister and legislators take great deal of interest in the transfers and postings of even non gazetteed officers so that they get officers of their own cast or pliable men are posted in their respective constituencies. This tendency of debasement has hit hard the moral of bureaucracy. Heads of the Department and district officers resisting political interference are either bullied, or humiliated[21] and finally they are given insignificant assignments. In an era of coalition government, this malady has gone deeper. Chief Minister in different states (and for that matter even in the Center) Prime Ministers have become prisoners in the hands of conflicting political parties and groups. To survive in office they are obliged to placate numerous petty politicians. The new breed of ministers with tenuous tenures are always on the lookout for pliable bureaucrats. There is no shortage of unprincipled opportunities in the bureaucracy. A large number of civil servants are aligned with particular ministers, become active and prove nexus collaborators, leading to formation of Political groups and the process consideration of seniority, merit, competence and integrity have been progressively marginalized, which has resulted in to various types of growth over the years. Bureautic growth of this Malignant Syndrome, embodying pervasive corruption, criminalization and electoral malpractice. The noxious socio-political has facilitated the emergence of high profile cynical politician with no faith in the constitution, the laws of the land and basic tenets of democracy. They look upon electoral victory as license to abuse power, help cronies and amass huge wealth. The brazen disregard further laid down policies rule and procedures has progressively eroded the functioning in the administrative system. The total absence of transparency and accountability in our system has facilitated these tragic developments in the governance of the country.[22] It is due to this kind of prevailing political culture even suggested measures such as citizen focus and result orientation, the core strategy for good governance remains a quixotic project. The fate of the Lok Pal bill is the burning example of the lack of Political will to check corruption. The Lok Pal Bill has been before the Parliament for three decades. Different Political parties have occupied the treasury benches. But bill remains to take shape of statute. Although amendments have been proposed from time to time but by and large the bill still remains dysfunctional.[23]

It is now indisputably true that corruption, politician bureaucratic-mafia nexus, criminalisation of politics very profoundly impinge upon the process of governance in the country. Due to these maladies quality of governance has gone down from the apex to the grass root level. Corruption, delay, harassment and impolite behaviour with people, lukewarmness of Public servants towards their duties are, in brief, the empirical reality of Indian governance system today.

As regards the containment of corruption in the functioning of the Political executive in the states and the need to secure greater efficiency and accountability of the governmental functionaries, there have been lengthy debates within and outside the parliament for past two decades. High-level commissions were instituted to streamline the functioning of the government, and to reform the election processes. So much so that the Supreme Court of India issued directions to the election commission in 2002 to prevent the criminals from contesting elections. All these efforts did not yield any positive result.

Then what is the remedy? How to secure the objective of good governance, accountability and transparency is the moot point in any discourse on good governance. Efforts towards civil service reforms in the past emphasized on securing leadership for change. It was acknowledged that the commitment of ministers and senior official to administrative reform programmes is quite important. Institutionalization within the governance machinery of the skills is necessary for the continuation and development of good management in government, should be they strategy if civil service reforms are to be carried out. But these goals cannot be attained unless there is a genuine political will and intent. There is evidence to prove this fact that the most successful reforms in U.K., Malaysia, Singapore and New Zealand were politically driven at the highest level.[24] The Business Management theories and techniques and strategies cannot be transplanted to system of governance without taking into account the political ambience of public administration in India. Unless nexus between politics and administration and the politician in power and civil servant is eliminated any remedy to streamline governance will be worse than the disease.

To conclude, it may be submitted that for securing the objective of good governance emphasis on accountability, transparency, commitment etc. are not enough. These are mere processes of good governance. A viable strategy of good governance must be relevant and should be capable of addressing sustainable human development and enjoyment of human rights with positive support of the political leadership.

References

1. K.P. Jaiswal, *Hindu Polity*, Bangalore Print and Publishing Co. 1968. P.40.See
2. V.P. Verma, *Ancient and Medieval Indian Political thought,* Laxmi Narain Agarwal, Agra,.
3. *Ibid.* p 39 कृत शतसहस्त्र हिश्लोकानामिदुमुदमत्रयम् लोकतंत्रस्य कृत्सनस्य यस्माद धर्मः प्रवर्तते cited by V.P. Verma from Santiparva, 335, 39.
4. *Ibid.*
5. तस्माच्छास्त्रं प्रमाणं ते कार्या कार्ये व्यवस्थिता ज्ञात्वा शास्त्र विहनोकृं कर्म कर्तु मिर्हाहसि The Gita, Chapter XVI verse 24. cited by O.P. Dwivedi in Common Good and Good Governance, *The Indian Journal of Public Administration,* Vol XLIV No.3 July-September 1998 p 259
6. O.P.Dwivedi No.5 p,254
7. See George Catlin, *A History of Political Philosophy,* Unwin, London, 1950, p 43.
8. See Aristotle's *Politics* Book VII, 4 p. 294
9. G.H. Sabine, *A History of Political Theory*, IBH Publication New Delhi, 1987, p. 220
10. P.K. Basu, *Towards a New Managerial Order in Asia*, Macmillan 1981 p. 42
11. N.N. Vohra, The Matrix of Governance, *South Asia Politics*, May 2002, (Inaugural issue) p.9

12. Ashok Mukhopadhyay, Reinventing Government for good governance, *The Indian Journal of Public Administration*, Vol. XLIV No.3 July-September 1998 p-282.

13. Mohit Bhattacharya, conceptualizing Good. Governance. *The Indian Journal of Public Administration*, VOL XLIV No 3, July-September 1998 P-291.

14. See *World Bank governance*, The world Bank's Experience, Washington, World Bank, 1944 PXIV.

15. See Michael Camdessus, Address to the United Nations, *Economic and Social Council* July 2, 1997.

16. Jack Boorman, The Role of the LMF in Governance Issues. *Guidance Note,* July25, 1997.

17. Neerja Gopal Jayal, The Governance Agenda: Making Democratic Development Dispensable, *Economic and Political weekly.*

18. See 'John Samuel, What is good governance, *Info-change India News Features Analysis File*, November 2004 p.p. 1-4.

19. N.S. Gehlot, Meaning of Good Governance and Its Relevance in the Functioning of Indian Democracy, *South Asia Politics*, Vol. 3 No. 2 Jun, 2003 p.14.

20. G. Narendra Kumar. An Institutional Framework for Good Governance in India. *P.L.* (Paper acquired through internet)

21. P.S. Appu, The All India Service, Declive, Debasement and Destruction. *Economic and Political weekly*, February 26, 2005 p. 828-830

22. *Ibid.*

23. S.R. Mohnot, Good Governance. The Missing Link in the Political Value Chain, *South Asia Politics*, Vol. 1. No. 7, November 2002 P.15

24. Mohan Kaul, Civil Service Reforms Learning from common wealth Experiences. *The Indian Journal of Public Administration*, Vol. XLIV No.3 July-September 1998 P. 689

8

Ideology Free Political Parties and Valueless Politicians: A Dangerous Trend for Good Governance

S. N. Mishra and Chaitali Pal

The search for good governance is a continuous and endless process. To ensure 'goodness' in governance and raising its level could be possible only when the aspirations of the people are taken care of and such aspirations are constantly articulated by all the sections of the society. However, good governance may be articulated differently by different scholars and individuals. For Bentham, good governance means satisfaction of every kind and full of pleasure. To quote him 'it is better to be a pig satisfied than to be a Socrates dissatisfied.' To put it differently, for Bentham, satisfaction is everything and, perhaps, rationality has no place in his thinking. Whereas J. S. Mill. makes a clear cut difference between the rational and irrational. Criticizing Bentham on rationality ground he says, 'it is always better to be a socrates dissatisfied than to be a pig satisfied'. Therefore, for J. S. Mill. good governance stands for rationality, individual freedom, liberty with checks and balances and transparency in governance.

Before Bentham and J. S. Mill, Hobbes, Locke and Rousseau treated state, as a result of social contract, synonymous to good governance. For Mahatma Gandhi, good governance means dignity of human being, value based society, self-restraint, dignity of labor and egalitarian society. Therefore, in India during the entire tortuous course of the freedom struggle, self- government and good governance became synonymous. After independence ,the Constitution which we adopted, the preamble of it sets forth the parameters for good governance.

However, the concept of good governance as envisaged in the Preamble of the Constitution and the searches for the seemingly elusive goal of good governance. It started with securing rights of common man in the Constitution through the provision of Fundamental Rights and the Directive Principles Of State Policy. However the guiding spirit, of course, has been the Preamble of the Constitution.

Good governance, however, is not a finished product. It is a dynamic concept. It encompasses fast changing political, social and economic milieu along with international environment and condition of operational governance. Hence, the need for periodical rethinking on and even remodeling of the concept and institutions of governance. The wide spread misgivings and apprehensions generated due to the gloomy scenario in recent past about the future of democratic functioning of our governmental system, and challenges further posed by the rising influence of international organizations have attracted greater attention of academics, public administrators and the common citizenry to look into various facets of good governance a fresh.[1]

When we talk about good governance, to our mind, it encompasses in its fold,

(i) Political institutions within which management is exercised with a focus on how the democratic institutions function. (ii) The authority and working of judiciary (iii) The administrative system and culture (iv) The role of civil society (v) Underlying socio-political dynamics which conditions the functioning of the above institutions.[2]

When one examines the above mentioned conditions, he finds that all the five areas influence the governance of a country. However, again the vexing problem with regard to theoretical constructs arises and that is the problem of prioritisation of a process of governance reform. Intuitively one may argue that specific dynamics of each region of India assigns varied weights to each of these issues. Therefore a common mosaic is required to develop a coherent and conceptual framework so as to enable us to study and spell out the determinants of good governance for the country. And as such when we talk about governance, it is itself an instrumental process designed to enable a society to realize certain objectives enshrined in the Constitution of the country. Therefore, without entering into an argument about the yardsticks to measure good governance we should take - note of following facts into account.

(a) Extent of deprivation - This measure moves beyond the conventional measure of GDP growth or even the human development indicators to encompass the issues of poverty and distribution. An appropriate measure of good governance would thus appear to be the extent to which a society has eliminated poverty, broadened access to entitlements and provided the basis for a sustainable livelihood for all its citizens . Here it must be emphasized that in putting deprivation at the center of our concern, we recognize that persistence of poverty deprives as much from deficiencies of economic policies. And therefore, it is the institutions of governance which in turn determine the implementation of development policies and influence its results

(b) Representativeness of representative institutions - It is accepted that ours is a representative government whose basic postulates are free and fair periodic elections both for Parliament and State Legislatures as also for the decentralized institutions of governance. However, it is open to challenges. Right from the independence till date, by and large, it has been noticed that be it the Parliament or the State Legislatures and for that matter the local representative bodies, there appear to be evidence that people of affluence dominate elective institutions even after reservation of seats for deprived sections of the society. It is rare for the poor to be able to contest the elections let alone get elected.

Since large number of population remains poor and the failure of the poor to be represented in representative bodies is a reality, this is perhaps one of the indicators of non-representativeness of our representative institutions. This may be seen as failure of governance relating both to the working of the democratic institutions and to development policy. Therefore, the failure of governance permits such an inequitable distribution of entitlements that it effectively excludes the poor from participation in legislatures. Such an exclusive system of representation is certainly undemocratic and serves to perpetuate inequitable policies and institutions.

(c) Decentralization of Governance-This yardstick looks at good governance in terms of how far political as well as administrative powers have been decentralized. For this we have to look into the process of decentralization, the nature of legislation, revenue resource and expenditure powers, as well as the nature and hierarchy of administration.

(d) Realization of basic and Fundamental Rights - If fundamental and basic rights of citizens are being sustained and protected and are seen as an end in itself as also an aspect of good governance, this suggests that India has been exposed to a process of usurpation of citizen's rights in the way of access to entitlements, health care, education, equality before the law and various freedoms. However, large segments of our population live in want and remain exposed to the arbitrary exercise of bureaucratic and public power. Therefore, some measure will need to be provided, based on the agreed definition of what constitutes fundamental and basic rights as well as equality before the law, to serve as a measure of good governance.

(e) Protection of Security of Life And Liberty-Good governance is judged on the basis of the extent to which security of life and liberty of our citizen is protected. This is a matter of concern because throughout the country the citizen is exposed to a life of insecurity owing to presence of armed people willing to use such arms to mobilize power and resources. The Ranveer Sena and the Lorik Sena of Bihar are few such examples. Apart from the coercive powers of police and military, citizen is also exposed to the dangers of the terrorists, noted criminals and Mafias. In other words lumpens rule over the security of common citizens. To a certain extent our judiciary also has not been very effective in setting the system right to ensure good governance. The judicial intervention in the kidnapping of film star Raj Kumar may be taken as exception.[3]

The above five measures of good governance prepare platform to inform all our subsequent analysis of the nature of public system in our country with particular reference to institutions of democracy. The Central argument of this piece of research is that good governance depends upon effective and representative character of our democratic institutions and enlightened citizens.

The title of this paper itself suggests that in the broader framework for good governance our specific concern is to examine the role and ethical values maintained by various political parties in the governance of the country. Such institutions are needed to give both voice and participation to citizens in the process of governance and to hold both the legislature and executive accountable and finally to prepare platform for good governance. If we define political process it can be said that political process is a way out to sort out the means and to chart the way towards the goal. It is an index and an instrument of dynamics of democracy through which qualitative changes occur. It is one of the crucial indices by which one may attempt to measure as to how far democracy as a value for good governance has been internalized among the political elite and the masses. Thus, it constitutes the mechanism for communication, influence and control from grassroots upwards The mechanisms involves both the political parties and the voters; one for materializing the public welfare programs and other for institutionalizing the people's will.[4]

The heart beat of a democratic political system is largely regulated by the sound health of political parties. Political parties not only channelise the political process during elections through nomination and campaign but also set forth the political goal and provide incentives to the citizen for political participation.

The focus of this article is on analyzing as to what extent periodic elections to Parliament and State Legislatures have set forth the process of good governance on the right track, as to whether the emerging electoral trends are any indicator of stability and viability of our political system, a 'sine-qua-non' of good governance, as to whether election reflect the institutionalisation of citizen's will; to assess the extent to which our Parliamentary system has sustained the test of the time and has helped in good governance and, finally, if the answer is in negative, to examine the measures required to be adopted to enable our political system ,to sustain the emerging challenges flowing from criminalisation of politics, liberalization of economy and erosion in administrative and judicial system. However, for the analysis purpose our basic concern is limited to the nomination process of the candidates of different political parties and its overall impact on good governance.

Before analysing the nomination process of the candidates for general election by various political parties, here we may add that selection of candidates by the parties is nomination and selection of candidates by the voters is election. Nomination is a supplimentary but most crucial process of election. If election is a competition among political parties, nomination process is a competition within the party amongst its members aspiring for contesting the election One represents inter-party competition, another stands for intra-party competition. Through this competition the inherent tendencies and attitudes of political parties are exposed to citizens. Through nomination process, political parties confine the choice of voters to the limited candidates and the motives behind the nomination of candidates pervade throughout the electoral fray and thereby effecting the working of Parliamentary government and setting forth the agenda for good governance.[5]

It not only determines the number, quality and ideology of candidates appearing at the hustings but also shapes the main contours of electoral fray. To be precise, the emerging trend of Indian Parliamentary system are to a great extent an outcome of nomination politics. However, to understand its futuristic trends in our Parliamentary system we have to peep into the past.

Since 1952, in successive three elections, values, ideology, commitment and integrity of the candidate ran supreme in the nomination process of various political parties. Irrespective of Ruling or Opposition all political parties authorised only those candidates to contest the elections whose party allegiance, loyalty and ideological commitment was beyond doubt. By and large, these candidates were involved in freedom movement and had their own good image in the public life.[6] These committed and ideology based politicians, after their election to respective State Legislatures and Parliament, prepared a sound platform for good governance of the country which was praised even by the foreigners like Paul Appelby, Moris Jones, Bailey and others. During those days the nomination process of the candidates used to start from the Taluka level coming to District and State level respectively and finally for the consideration of party high command.

However, in mid 60's, particularly after the death of Pundit Jawaharlal Nehru and with the emergence of coalition politics, ideology based nomination of candidates took the back seat for the first time which resulted into increasing interference by the Central leadership and gradually denying the effectiveness of democratic functioning of political parties at the State level and below. So long Nehru was alive bossism could not come in the way of democratic process of nomination of candidates of his party as he always tried to maintain harmony among different units of party organisation. He gave due importance to constituency units in the selection of candidates and encouraged to bring popular and allegiant members in the electoral fray belonging to both right and left wings of the party.[7]

During this period the Opposition parties, in the absence of tough competition among the ticket seekers, conferred tickets only on those candidates who had their own standing in the constituency as also in the national and state politics through their clean image and social and political services, thus providing a solid base for good governance. This was the period during which two major progressive forces, Socialist Party and Communist Party of India witnessed vertical splits in their ranks giving birth to Praja Socialist Party, and Socialist Party, Communist Party of India and Communist Party Marxists respectively and Akhil Bharatiya Jana Sangha was also gaining ground.

However, unfortunately after the sad demise of Pandit Jawaharlal Lal Nehru, in the Fourth General Elections of 1967, Congress faced with internal quarrel and leaders of both right and left wings of the party endeavoured to hold Congress command in their own hands at the cost of party ideology and personal integrity and therefore the party organisation was weakened and became dependent on faction and caste oriented provincial leadership.[8]

On the other hand, the growing concern and anxiety of Opposition parties, to oust the Congress from power, laid them to forge anti- congress alliance and absorb the Congress left-overs in their parties. As a result, anti-congress grand alliance deprived many competent party workers of the tickets in their respective constituencies and strong holds. At the same time the emerging rural elite also tried to spread their tentacles on faction ridden and ideology free political parties. Therefore, the party membership became either nonexistent or dead, leaving the way wide open for authoritarian dictates from the leading personalities and, ultimately, nomination of candidates virtually became a trial of strength among different personalities at the top.[9] As a result, *'leaving aside the party and national interests, Legislators got motivated towards committing political sin of defection, re-defection and counter-defection'**, and therefore the concept of strong Opposition and stable government became a distant possibility, if not permanently at least for the time being.

For a brief period *i.e.,* during 1971-77, trend towards non ideological membership, immense increase in number of defectors and emergence of Mrs. Indira Gandhi as unchallenged leader of the country, provided scope for personalised politics in the guise of caste, creed, communalism and regionalism. Therefore, during 1971 election both the Indira Congress and Opposition parties nominated the candidates for elections based on individual dominance. In other words, the candidates who had proved their loyalties to the top leadership of the party were rewarded with party tickets. Thus Party allegiance and the ideological commitment of the candidates did not play any decisive role at the time of distribution of tickets. The electoral outcomes did not prove to be a good trend for good governance. And this trend afterwards led towards money bag politics and use of muscle power.

Inspite of the success of Nav Nirman Movement in Gujrat and J.P. Movement in Bihar as also the nightmare of emergency, the Opposition parties though polarised at the time of election were intrenched in personalised politics. And therefore at the time of distribution of tickets, leaders became more important than the parties. It was because, the Janata party which emerged in the wake of emergency was an amalgamation of six parties. In this context J.K. Baral's case study rightly suggests that who was more powerful or close to those who were powerful within the party was beneficiary of nomination politics at the cost of another who normally should have got the ticket.[10] The end result of the 1977 electoral battle had been highly unsatisfactory and *'the people's aspirations of good governance seemed belied.'** It is because, perhaps, the personalised politics within the Janata Party laid to its downfall.

In the mid-term Parliamentary election of 1980 along with other prevailing factors, nomination politics tilted towards encouraging family dominance in the political process of the country. All most all the top leaders, with a few exceptions, successfully manipulated to reward with tickets their family members and close relatives without considering their ideological affinity and political standing in politics.[11] Similarly, in the Assembly election of 1980 the final arbitrators of ticket distribution managed to distribute the tickets in such a way that old bossism and factionalism could be thwarted giving way to some new equations and changes. The Times of India called it a generational change and "India's cultural revolution." Therefore this time there was a marked departure from the usual pattern of selection of candidates as no body could take nomination for granted. Nobody's entrenched claim seemed to have been recognised. Many of those who held seats in dissolved House had been ignored for some reason or other.[12]

According to political Pandits, there was no real issue in 1984 election, and a pro-Hindu, anti-sikh, backlash brought Rajiv Gandhi in power but no body really made a micro analysis of this hypothesis. After all, 1984 by all accounts was supposed to be a very bad year for Mrs. Gandhi's era of decisive leadership. It was, in a sense, coming to an end. Under the circumstances mentioned above the nomination politics in 1984 election did not set any new trend.

However, during the election of 1989-90, gambler seemed to have folded his cards. The Mr. Clean (Rajiv Gandhi) of 1984 had acquired a new title in 1989, *i.e.,* Mr. Safe. The return of old coterie to the fold indicated a return of wheeler dealer and musclemen to the ruling party and bringing of the end of the reformist process Rajiv Gandhi initiated in the winter of 1984.[13]

If we look into the nomination strategies of Opposition Parties, it appears that (1977-1989) occasionally they displayed rare unity with a one to one contest against the Congress in most of the constituencies. The Opposition appeared to be in upbeat mood. The atmosphere, the faces, the vibes were all familiar and so was the challenge. Therefore the United Front partners took to maneuvering and counter-maneuvering tactics to extract maximum seats. In nutshell, the 1989 election was fought on two basic cards *i.e.,* social justice card of V. P. Singh and Mandir card of L.K.Advani and therefore the society was divided between 'Mandal' and 'Kamandal' . In this election a new trend was noticed and that was the appearance of underworld prominently on the political scene veering round the two issues. After this election too no positive trend was set for good governance by various political parties.

The mid-term elections of 1991 were fought on three major planks-the Congress played its old card of stability and development, the left front democratic front combined played the card of social justice, whereas the B.J.P. raised the issue of Ayodhya Mandir. This strategy was clearly reflected in the nomination of candidates for the election of Lok Sabha and the State Legislatures. In the list of BJP nominees, the activities of

Vishva Hindu Parishad, the Sadhus and Sadhavis figured prominently. Similarly, the list of candidates of left- front, democratic-front combined was dominated by backward Castes, Muslims, Scheduled Castes and Scheduled Tribes. The Congress again depended upon the money and muscle power of the State strongmen. The basic concern of all political parties was to select such candidates who could match in money and muscle power of their counter parts.

The election of 1996, 1998, 1999, also set the same trend and criminalisation of politics and muscle power had been the hot matter of debate among the Psephologists at the time of elections. Thus looking into nomination process of political parties, in the historical perspectives, what appears to be the rising phenomena are; corruption not only in high places but in the whole of the body politic, gangsterism, repression, institutional decay, politics of survival, personality cult, emergence of Mafias and Dadas, rise of Facism and erosion of the State. Unfortunately these trends are very dangerous, so far good governance is concerned. Here, we would like to mention that it is better only to use the word 'governance' than to use 'good governance'. To our mind, governance itself stands for everything *i.e.,* social harmony, corruption free society, value based politics, free and fair elections, committed bureaucracy, decentralisation of power, transparency in governance, dissemination of knowledge, equity, neutrality of civil services, concern for the poorest of the poor, access to education, health, shelter, clothing and information to all, dignity of labour and finally enlightened citizens.

All these trends are slowly but gradually attacking on system of governance and subverting our administrative and judicial system. For example, a new culture among politicians which has developed in regard to bureaucracy is called 'My man and His man'. This phenomena has, to a great extent, affected the bureaucratic functioning and has brought the spoil culture, to which, the Americans said 'good bye' long ago.

To explain it further we would like to quote the discussion on the Zee T.V. in Prime Time News (at 9.30 P.M. dated Sep 28, 2000) in which two D.G.P., one from Rajasthan and another from Uttar Pradesh, were taking part in discussion and the topic of discussion was 'image of police bureaucracy.' One of the discussants, Mr. Gupta, the DGP of Rajasthan pointed out that due to political interference the average tenure of a Superintendent of Police during the last nine years in U.P. has been three months sixteen days. Same is applicable in case of civil bureaucracy. Similarly the judiciary is also not left unaffected. The action of the then Chief Minister of Haryana, Shri Bhajan Lal, influencing the High Court judge in O.P. Jindal's case and annoyance expressed by the Supreme

Courts[14] are some of the few examples of this nature. As regards political interference in judicial process, there has been a rising trend and barely goes a day, without coverage of such type of interference in the National News Papers. However, of late, judiciary has tried to intervene effectively in checking the corrupt practices of the Legislature and Executive. The judgement of the special court on Sep. 29, 2000, in Jharkhand Muktimorcha bribe case may be treated as a landmark in this direction, as a subordinate judiciary has punished the Former Prime Minister of the country, Shri P. V. Narasimha Rao and the then important minister, Shri Buta Singh.

The politics of expediency and self-survival in nomination process of Political Parties has brought them to a stage where they have lost their homogenous character and institutional norms. If casteism, communalism and regionalism have disrupted the value oriented and ideology based composition of political parties, induction of hat changers and unscrupulous politicians has damaged their representative character. Political parties either in power or in opposition face a common threat in the form of militant movements of various special interest groups, thus making them incapable of harmonizing social conflicts, attenuate regional distance and protect collective interest. And as such, they have badly failed in harmonizing and integrating the people's hopes and aspirations, which is a basic prerequisite of good governance.

Distancing them from party ideology, the political parties in nomination of candidates right from the First General Election till date, have failed to set forth the process of Parliamentary democracy on the right track and are gradually becoming a shelter house of self seekers and power seekers. A sound mechanism of communication, influence and control from grass-root level upward is yet another prerequisite of good governance, but the trends from various elections reflects that the political parties have failed in developing such mechanism. At the same time, they have also failed in institutionalising people's will. The emerging trends also do not indicate stability for a Parliamentary system. Politics has become varitable profession where all that matters is an elective seat. The ticket based patronization and personalised politics has almost destroyed the very 'raison d' etre' of the election and has left the political parties in the position of by- stander, putting tremendous pressure on the political system which is not good for governance as a whole. In such a situation all the political parties, national or regional, are required to build such a cadre of theirs' which should be ideologically committed having a mission to serve the people and honest to the core. Some legal provisions are also required to regulate the functioning of political parties and their cadre. In order to put a check on the criminalisation of politics, the law should also provide a provision that no candidate either convicted or being tried is allowed to contest the election.

Finally, in order to strengthen the role of political parties, the practice of bloating of Council of Ministers must be stopped and the party should develop think tanks within their organisations to come up with alternative policy proposals to smoothen the process of governance.[15]

It has almost become an accepted fact that coalitional politics has come to stay in India at least for coming two decades. This experiment has succeeded in many western countries and there is nothing wrong in it. However, the deficiency lies in the way we have worked in and part of blame must be shared by both political parties and political leadership. The political parties have to take into account, the inherent diversity of the country and at all cost integrate such diversities to the maximum satisfaction of all, which is 'sin-qua-non' for good governance.

References

* The Italic is ours.

** The Italics is of authors.

1. Editorial, *Indian Journal Of Public Administration*, Special Number on 'Towards Good Governance' Vol. XLIV, July-Sept. 1999, PX, IIPA, New Delhi.
2. Rehman, Sobhan, '*Problems of Governance in South Asia: an overview*'. (Ed.) V.A. Paipanandikar, Konark Publishers, New Delhi, 2000, p. 2.
3. Mishra, S.N. and Pal, Chaitali, ' Good governance: the context of democratic decentralisation (ed) Suresh Mishra, in "Essays in public Administration", *Sustainable Development Foundation*, New Delhi, 2000.
4. Mishra, S.N. And Mishra, Sweta. 'Political process and political parties in India: Retrospect and prospect' in *IJPA*, VOL. XL. NO. 3, July-Sep. 1994.
5. *Ibid.*
6. Mishra and Mishra, *op.cit.*
7. W.H. Morris Jones, *The government and politics in India*, London, Hutchinson, 1971, p. 92.
8. Iqbal Narayan, *'Twilight or dawn', The political change in India, (1967-71)*, Agra, Shivlal, 1972, pp. 35-36.
9. L.N. Sharma, "Selection of candidates by political parties in Bihar for mid-term Parliamentary Poll 1971", *Journal of Constitutional and Parliamentary Studies*, Jan-Mar, 1980.
10. L.N. Sharma, *op.cit.*
11. *India Today*, Dec. 16-31, 1979, p. 72.

12. *Northern India Patrika*, May 19, 1980.

13. *India Today*, Nov. 19-30, 1989.

14. *The Times of India*, New Delhi, July, 22, 1994.

15. Jain, R.B., 'Review of the working of the Indian Constitution: an agenda for reform of the party system,' paper presented at the *General Body Meeting of I.I.P.A.* Delhi Regional Branch, dated, 26, month missing 2000, p. 7.

9

Politician-Bureaucrate Relationship: A Good Governance Perspective

D. P. Chaturvedi

A political system adopts a particular pattern depending upon several factors including historical and immediate. For instance in U.K. Parliamentary system came in existence as a result of historical struggle between the monarch and the people.

To-day the advocates of parliamentary system support it because it secures an essential co-operation, co-ordination and harmony between legislature and executive which lead to administrative efficiency.

Each society imparts its own characteristic set on norms and values to its people. In India the political system has established its administrative process on the British pattern. Under the guidance of political executive rules are implemented by a professional bureaucracy. In that set up 'CABINET SECRETARY' is the crown authority.

It is crystal clear that we have planned a welfare state in which public interest is supreme. Although the parliamentary form by self is not an index of the democracy, yet all parliamentary systems have in common a close institutional relationship between the executive and parliament. Each Minister is responsible for administering a particular department of Govt.

Modern democracies are faced with a problem which has arisen out of the large population and complex organisation that modern life has evolved. The problem always is "Good Governance" and how the rule of the people should function in actual practice, leadership and governance of a democracy in the modern age has undergone a vast change.

The key component of 'governance' were identified in the policy directive of the OECD documents as follows:

- Legitimacy of Govt;
- Accountability of Political and official elements of Govt;

- Competence of govt. to make policy and deliver services;
- Respect for human rights and rule of Law.

Before centuries Maharishi Ved Vyas wrote in the Mahabharata "Yugasya Cha Çhaurthasya Raja Bhawati Karnam".

Maharshi Valmiki too gave much importance to the morality of the king. It is a reality that the character of the king has been always a point of discussion among the subject. The subject as a whole were responsible to him and the himself was morally responsible to him. In the same Way even to-day the administration and officials of the state had legal and moral responsibility. It shows a clear accountability in ancient India.

After Independence again we were face to face with the same problem of morality in the govt. and administration. After Independence we got the leaders who had popular appeal to the masses and also a strong and decisive political and administration skill. Gradually those leaders were away from the national scene. The new political generation is anxious to interfere the administration at all levels. In later year this "Political intervention", created uneasiness in bureaucracy.

Here I am analysing this "Political invention" which is a greatest obstacle in running the administration smoothly.

Now the question arises, what is intervention? Where political leader pressurises the civil servant to act beyond law, against justice and public interest is 'intervention'. In such cases, the strong hand of Prime Minister is needed. Prime Minister should be in a position to control the Politicians as well as to the bureaucrats. Otherwise "good-governance" cannot be achieved.

In this very reference we shall have to make difference between "control over administration" and "intervention in the administration". Former is necessary while later is unwanted.

In responsible system of govt. administration is in better position in comparison with govt. because bureaucrats are selected for a long span of time. They are professionals too.

Employee-employer relationship is a very sensitive matter. It depends over the efficiency and working of both sides. If one is weaker the other will be stronger. Practical knowledge and mass appeal are the real strength of the political leader.

Ex-British Prime Minister Lord Atlee had these qualities. When a high official advised him to introduce a control over 'coal and kerosene', he pathetically replied—' Where will they keep it? 'When I was in East London I used to keep it under my bed.'

The real strength and political power of the Politician rests here. This sort of practical wisdom gives the upper hand to the Minister.

According to democratic norms if any wrong goes in some department Minister should be taken for granted, not the civil servant.

Lord George Boown says, "If something is going wrong shoot the Minister." If the Minister is not satisfied with the advice of his bureaucrat, it is his problem that how to handle the bureaucrat.

Minister has power to appoint, transfer or expel the civil servant. In India transfer is "very cheap and popular punishment". Neutrality, which has been a very strong character of Indian Civil Service, is under-pressure. This 'punishment-tactic' is gradually leading them towards frustration. So, the opportunists are seeking the shelter of some influential umbrella.

I remember those days when Sri Abdul Rehman Antuley was the Chief Minister of Maharashtra. He transferred a higher official thrice a year only because he was not obeying his illegal orders 'word by word'. Such examples are easily available in other states too.

Later a new development of 'committed bureaucracy' has come in existence. During the long tenure as P.M. Mrs. Indira Gandhi tried her best to force the official to kneel down. 'Prisoners of conscience' were punished. She created a cacus of committed bureaucrats around her. A large portion of bureaucracy found itself helpless in new conditions.

The British pattern which we have opted for the civil service is conservative in its attitude and traditional in its behaviour. It shows less enthusiasm to the progressive steps of the govt. To-day in India the pubic image of bureaucracy is one of inaccessibility, indifference, procedure-orientation, poor quality and sluggishness, corruption proneness and non-account ability for results. On the contrary the need of the day is an efficient, accountable and clear administration at all levels.

Now the another question arises—Whether they civil servants should be free from the control of Politicians? Will it be proper for 'good governance'? The answer will be "Certainly not". The control of the Minister over administration is the soul of the Parliamentary system. A proper co-ordination between both organs strengthens the polity while rivalry will generate disorder and indiscipline. To avoid, political anarchy and establish discipline is the demand of the day.

Another factor that is an obstacle on the way of 'good governance' is corruption. It is deep rooted in government as well as in the administration. It seems that an unpious coalition of leaders, bureaucrat and mafia has come in existence.

A move to inspire honest administrators and to whip corrupt one is initiated by Mr. N. Vittal. He has displayed the names of corrupt bureaucrats on the internet (media). It has created a sense of admiration for his act. This should be widened. The public is supporting this step. In an inaugural speech at I.A.S. Association gathering he suggested them to name "Top Ten" corrupt officers for the betterment of the image of the administrative services.

At present the reliability of a political persons like—Anna Hajare, Khairnar, Medha Patekar or Sheshan has increased. Virtually corruption on high levels have created a history. It is developing like infectious disease and political leaders has become dwarf.

Bofors, Telecom, Gaurantee, Sugar, Hawala and Fodder Episodes have created a sense of uneasiness in the public. A "Vittal-like" move also be started in political corruption too.

Indian constitution is a well-drafted document ensuring freedom with justice. The fundamental righs provide for not only individual rights but also certain social rights to the down-trodden. The principle of protective dissenmination is accepted, which is a move towards equality of opportunity. To some extent constitution admits the fact society in which it has to operate is 'unjust' and 'unqeual'. In this case purpose of governance is clearly laid down that the governance has to be in favour of charging the context and also the content of socio-political processess.

Summing up, the urgent need of the time is to bring about reforms in administration to make it proactive, accountable and efficient.

References

1. *The World Bank*, Governance and Development, Washington DC (1972).
2. *Conference* of Chief Secretaries (1996) of India.
3. O.E.C.D. Countries *Report*.
4. John Rawls, *A Theory of Justice*, Harward University Press, 1971.
5. Mohit Bhattacharya, "Conceptualising Good Governance". *Seminar*, Political Science Dept. Meerut University.
6. D.D. Basu, *Introduction to the Constitution of India*, New Delhi, Prentice Hall.
7. Moriss, Jones, *The Govt. and Politics of India*, Hutchinson University Library, London, (1967).
8. C.P. Bhambri, *Public Adminstration in India*.
9. C. Subramanyam, Representative Bureaucracy—A Re-assessment, *The American Political Science Review*.
10. Shanti Kothari & Ramasray Rai, *Relation between Politicians and Administrator*.
11. R.B. Jain, *Contemporary Issues in Indian Administration*.

10

Good Governance and Human Rights: The Indian Perspective

Jaytilak Guha Roy

The late 20th Century globalisation has brought about a paradigm shift in the "nature and character" of the state and public administration from "the traditional welfare administrative state to a corporate welfare state."[1] Under the grab of promoting the cause of liberal democracy, the international and western aid-giving agencies, like World Bank and OECD countries, seem to have been encroaching upon sovereignty of the Third World countries, their right to development, and forcing them to accept a revised version of the gospel of capitalism. Consequently, many few concepts or ideals have suddenly entered the vocabulary of public administration—Privatisation, Public Service Management, Good Governance, to name a few.[1]

Prima facie these new concepts or ideals aim at reforms, and it is true that no nation can prosper, or even survive, without reforms from time to time in social, economic, administrative and various other fields. To quote Sir Edmund Burke, "A nation without the means of reforms is without means of survival." However, reform, to be meaningful, has to be well-planned, well-directed and above all, conducive to national needs and interests. Sadly, for a Third World country as ours, the agenda for reforms of the 1990s appear to have been imposed by international and western donor agencies rather than adopted by choice. And herein lies the dilemma of the ongoing process of reforms.

New Concept of Governance and its Operational Limitations

Traditionally, governance refers to forms of political system and the manner in which power is exercised in utilising country's economic and social resources for development.[2] Based on its lending experience in developing countries, the World has identified a number of political and administrative aspects of good governance such as:

- political accountability including the acceptability of political system by the people;
- freedom of association and participation by various religious, social, economic, cultural and professional groups in the process of governance;
- an established legal framework based on the rule of law and independence of judiciary to protect human rights, secure social justice and guard against exploitation and abuse of power;
- freedom of information and expression needed for formulation of public policies, decision-making, monitoring and evaluation of government performance;
- Cooperation between the government and civil society organisations.[3]

Donor agencies' attempt to prescribe an uniform model of governance seems to be unrealistic. In fact, there are genuine problems and limitations in operationalising the new concept of governance in actual practice. As one western scholar observes very forthright:

Like democracy, governance remain a particularly difficult variable to operationalise. At present 'good governance' is seemingly defined in terms of a *check-list of criteria* (transparency, accountability, public sector management, etc.) that governance must broadly satisfy in order to justify receiving loans. However, it is not made explicit which, if any, of these are prioritised and how they should be measured and compared. Governance is not a binary variable and cannot defined in terms of 'on/of', or 'present/absent' criteria.[4]

Costs of International Human Rights Activism

Respect for human rights and protection of human rights have been identified by international and western or agencies as some of the key components of 'governance'. Consequently, in recent years, there has been unnecessary proliferation of international human rights, the costs of which seem to be extremely unfair for the Third World nations. "As *rights*-oriented agendas increasingly dominate the politics and budgets of Western countries", observes a western critique very poignantly, "*human-rights* activism has expanded to exert pressure on nations around the world to assure greater governmental and social compliance with Western *human rights* standards." As this critique observes further, "The unbridled growth of *human rights* accentuates differences among persons and groups, threatens internal order and social cohesion, and transforms nations into mere states. In the worst cases the uncontrolled growth of *rights*, like *cancer* cells, can kill the hosts that nurture them—and thereby kill themselves."[5]

One may or may not agree with the above observations. Nevertheless, the fact remains that excessive emphasis on human rights by the donor agencies has been backfired to the extent that even the legitimate concern for human rights is now being looked upon with suspicion by a large chunk of educated citizens including civil bureaucracy in our country.

Fulfilling Our Human Rights Obligations

There is no denying that the demands of donor agencies for human rights compliance are irrelevant, inconsistent and incompatible. Nevertheless, it needs to be emphasised that India, being the signatory of the International Bill of Human Rights (IBHR) consisting of the 1948 Universal Declaration of Human Rights (UDHR), and the 1966 International Covenant on Civil and Political Rights and International Covenant on Economic, Social and Cultural Rights, has legal as well as moral obligations to adhere to minimum human rights standards laid down by IBHR. As the preamble to the UDHR declares unequivocally, "Human rights are a common standard of achievement for all peoples and all nations." Broadly speaking, human rights, as defined by an eminent scholar, "are internationally agreed values, standards or rules regulating the conduct of states towards their own citizens and towards non-citizens."[6]

It needs to be mentioned further that the first Indian Statute which defines "human rights" is *The Protection of Human Rights Act, 1993*. Under this Act, human rights means "the rights relating to life, liberty; equality and dignity of the individual guaranteed by the Constitution or embodied in the International Covenants and enforceable by courts in India." Hence, the major issue is: how to fulfil our obligations for human rights? The following are some of the measures suggested by this scribe:

Firstly, the right to life is essential for the enjoyment of human rights in the real sense. The right to life implies the right to live with dignity. This right can be ensured in a developing country as ours only when millions of our poor people will be provided with basic human needs such as food, clothing, housing, health and education. This calls for greater involvement of civil society organisations at the grass root level in implementation of poverty alleviation policies and programmes. These organisations should also act as the watchdog bodies to prevent misuse and diversion of funds in these programmes.

Secondly, there is an urgent need to ensure that the benefits of economic growth and industrial development percolate to the lowest strata of the society. In this sphere too, civil society organisations must act closely with the government and even private sector.

Thirdly, the economic policies and programmes of the government need to be suitably modified and enforced to protect and promote labour-intensive trades and enterprises including our indigenous crafts and products, and also to create job opportunities for youths with due emphasis on self-employment.

Last but not the least, any effort towards good governance would be futile unless administration is made transparent, responsive, efficient and accountable.

Concluding Observations

Increasing awareness of human rights in recent years has inevitably raised people's expectations. Failure to provide good governance would lead us to a much more turbulent society than we have today. Hence, the need of the hour is collaboration rather than confrontation between state and civil society organisations, between government and non-government sectors.

References

1. Au Farazmand, "Globalisation and Public Administration", *Public Administration Review*, 59 (6), Nov-Dec. 1999, p.510.
2. Mick Moore, "Declining to Learn from the East: The World Bank on Governance and Development", *IDS Bulletin*, 24 (1), 1993, p.39.
3. Peter Blunt, "Cultural Relativism, Good Governance and Sustainable Human Development" *Public Administration and Development*, 15, 1995, pp.5-7.
4. Bob Currie, "Governance, Democracy and Economic Adjustment in India: Concept and Empirical Problem", *Third World Quarterly* 17 (4), 1996 (emphasis added).
5. John A. Gentry, "The Cancer of Human Rights", *Washington Quarterly*, Autumn 1999, 22 (4), p. 95, 18p.
6. Peter R. Baehr, *Human Rights: Universality in Practice*, London, Macmillan, 1999, p. 1.

11

Humanising Development: An Essence of Good Governance

A Peep in Human Development Reports

R. K. Wishwakarma

Introduction

In today's context of development, humanising development is the most challenging task of governments of all developing nations. It requires good governance. The test of good governance is to create an enabling environment for the people "to enjoy long, healthy and creative lives". It is in this direction that the governments in most of the developing countries of the world are continuously initiating and adopting a wide variety of measures for good governance and effective management for peoples demand for better services which is closely linked to the democratic decentralisation enhanced by social economic and gender equity through community's empowerment and capacity building. This is in the context that—"governments do not solve problems, people do".

To this end of humanising development poverty is a severe blockage. Provision of water sanitation and hygiene contribute significantly to elimination of poverty and often form an entry point to human development. In the existing scenario of development, the most inhibiting factor is the lack of synergy of action between different stakeholders and actors. This requires the efforts of a wide range of individuals, institutions and organisations. The Government of India (and government of all other developing nations too) are not only creating a wide variety of institutions and organisations but also involved very much in finding out ways and means of improving and institutionalising the already existing and newly created institutions, to make them effective instruments of human development. But the path of success lies in the collaboration-the way to greater synergy which requires mutual trust and understanding.

Concept of Human Development

The broad approach to improving human well-being would cover all aspects of human life, beyond narrowly defined economic development to cover the full flourishing of all human choices. It emphases, the need to put people their-needs, their aspirations and their capabilities at the center of development effort, irrespective of any biases.[1] Human development is the process of enlarging peoples choices not just choices among different detergents, television channels—what people do and can do in their lives. At all levels of development a few capabilities are essential for human development, without which many choices in life will not be available. These capabilities are to lead long and healthy lives, to be knowledgeable and to have access to the resources needed for a decent standard of living and these are reflected in the human development indices (discussed in the later part of this paper). But many additional choices are valued by people. These include political social, economic and cultural freedom, a sense of community, opportunity for being creative and productive an self-respect and human rights. Yet human development is more than just achieving these capabilities, it is also the process of pursuing them in a way that is equitable, participatory, productive and sustainable[2]. Human development thus has many dimensions.

Getting income with more increasing power is one dimension. Although it is important, yet not or all important option. It requires more than what development thinkers assume about them. In addition to more income, the poor people desire adequate food, nutrition, safe drinking water at hand, better medical services more and better schooling for their children, cheap transport, adequacy of shelter, continuing employment with security of livelihood and dignity of freedom of movement and speech, liberation from oppression, violence an exploitation, the assertion of cultural and religious values, adequate leisure and aesthetics and cultural development. These dimensions of human development are often more highly valued than income for which policies can create the opportunities for their fulfillment.

Human Development Reports-Opening New Vistas of Policy Development

Starting from the first Human Development Report (HDR) 1990, each year the HDR has been focussing on different themes and introduced new concepts and approaches but the people have been the concern of development. A balance sheet of human development during 1990-97 though shows tremendous progress, there have been enduring deprivations and new setbacks. Even then each year, Human Development Report has helped in opening near vistas of policy development debates for under possibilities.

The new paradigm of sustainable development of the Earth Summit 1992 advocated for sustainable human development to be in terms of (i) pro-people (ii) pro-job, and (iii) pro-nature. This led to the global proposals and new concepts of human security and a new partnership of developed and developing countries in term of the 20:20 INITIATIVE (1992). This initiative led to propose that each developing country should allocate 20% of its domestic budget and every donor 20% of its official development assistance (ODA) towards basic minimum services-ensuring basic health care, basic education, access to safe drinking water and environmental sanitation including family planning packages for all couples.

Creating Human security fund (1994) with $ 250 billion for tackling the problems of drug trafficking, international terrorism, communicable diseases, nuclear proliferation, natural disasters, ethnic conflicts, excessive international migration and global environmental pollution and degradation is another move towards pollution and degradation. In addition, a New Global Architecture (1994) came into being to deal with problems that nations alone cannot solve. These relate to the upcoming of an economic security council to review the threats to the human security; a world central bank-to take on global macroeconomic management and supervision of international banking; an international investment trust- to recycle international surpluses to developing countries; and a world antimonopoly authority to monitor the activities of multi-national corporations and ensure that markets are competitive.

Besides, as of December 1998, 163 nations of the world ratified the 1979 Convention on the elimination of all forms of Discrimination Against Women (1995) (CEDAW) advocating equality between women and men— all over the globe by 2005 within the framework of CEDAW. Following the international agenda of reforms on the above critical issues of global importance, the national proposals focussed on the need for near partnership between governments, institutions of civil society-and communities of people across the nations.

It was further agreed to restructure and reallocate resources to basic human priority concerns through an analysis of country's total expenditure social expenditure and human priority spending ratios. The pro-poor growth (1996) dimension of human development laid more emphasis on the quality of growth. It is as important as the quantity of growth. Human development growth should be "job-creating rather than jobless, poverty reducing rather than ruthless, participatory rather-than voiceless, culturally entrenched rather than rootless, and environment-friendly rather than futureless. A growth strategy that aims for a more equitable distribution of assets, that is job-creating and labour-intensive, and that is decentralised can achieve such growth"[3].

A Critical threshhold of 30% Gr., for Women's Representation (1995) in all decision making process: economic, political and social- nationally and locally is essential to enable women to influence decision making that affect their lives. This requires gender equality in all opportunities made equal to men's.

The Agenda for Poverty Eradication laid emphasis on empowerment as the key issue for poverty elimination with six-point agenda:

Empower individuals, households and communities to gain greater control over their lives and resources.

- Strengthen gender equality to empower women.
- Accelerate pro-poor growth in low-income countries.
- Improve the management of globalisation.
- Ensure an active state committed to eradicating poverty.
- Take special actions for special situations to support progress in the poorest and weakest countries.

Human Development—A tool for Influencing Policy

As a consequence of the impact of human development efforts of the UNDP, two Human Development Centres have been established—the first in Islamabad, Pakistan, and the second in Guanajuanto, Mexico. More than 260 reports have been prepared during the 1990-99 decade, by 120 nations, in addition to nine regional reports influencing national policies and mobilising community for equitable participatory, productive and sustainable development.

In India, many of 25 states unequal in size and diversity in population and resources hide the regional disparities at macro-level. UNDP India has therefore supported the preparation of human development by the state governments. The government of Madhya Pradesh has been the first State to have prepared a Sate Report in 1995 focussing human development in political discourse and planning. The 1998 Report reflects the impact of first report on planning. As a result, social services account for 42% of plan investment as compared to 19% in previous budgetary allocation. The success of human development report bodes well for other states like Gujarat, Karnataka and Rajasthan preparing their first human development report. The Government of Uttar Pradesh has also taken a decision to prepare a report on human development.

Understanding the importance of human development, South Africa also brought out critical gaps in information to light and the economic costs in terms of lost labour and sick days are estimated to be far more than initially realised.

Many other countries like Kuwait introduced the human development perspective and its relevance to the country's economy, made a policy shift from dependence on oil towards knowledge based economy. Guatemala's first human development report, 1998 highlighted socio-economic disparities across regions laid emphasis on the strengthening of national system of statistics and its information to civil society is a requirement for democracy. Latvia and Lithuania reports on human development covering the social effects of transition, human settlements, social collision and poverty have now inspired a cross-border academic network. Likewise, Cambodia's human development reports have provided unique overview of human development in a country where reliability of statistical information has been a major obstacle in developing sustainable social and economic policies. The 1998 report drew public attention to the persistent discrimination against women in access to education and health care. With the governments initiatives and participation of many NGOs, attempts are being made to strengthen local capacity in compiling and analysing data on human development.

Concept of Human Security

Human Development Report, 1994 presented the concept of human security which has two main aspects:

- Safety from such chronic threats: such as hunger, disease an repression
- Protection from sudden and hurtful disruptions in the patterns of daily life whether in homes, in jobs, or in communities. Such threats exists at all levels of national income and development.[5]

Threats to Human Security

There are many threats to human security, differing for individuals at different times, fall into seven main categories6:

- Economic insecurity
- Food insecurity
- Health insecurity
- Personal insecurity
- Environmental insecurity
- Community and cultural insecurity
- Political insecurity

The loss of human security can be a slow, silent process- or an abrupt land emergency. Humans can be at fault with bad policy choices so can the forces of nature. Or it can be a combination of the two-when environmental degradation ("a silent emergency") leads to a natural disaster, followed by human tragedy, scientists, predicts a steady rise in global temperatures and sea levels, inundating as much as 17% of the land area in Bangladesh, 12% in Egypt and almost all of the Maldives.

Leaving aside the non-renewable resources, even renewable resources are being depleted rapidly and unsustainable: fish stocks are estimated to be three quarters of what they once were. Water availability is 60% of 1970 levels, as is forest coverage. All this threatens and endangering economic security, food security and health security of the worlds poorest people.

Globalisation and Human Development

Although globalisation driven by commercial market forces expands opportunities for unprecedented human advancement in terms of "integration of economy, culture and governance", yet it misses out on the goals of equity poverty eradication and enhanced human security". Human Development requires social protection not only from nations but from communities, NGOs, Corporations and international cooperation. To pursue human development globalisation has to mean:

- "Ethics-less, not more violation of human rights and disregard of human values.
- Development-less, not more poverty of countries and people.
- Equity-less, not more disparity between and within nations an generations.
- Inclusion- less, not more marginalisation and exclusion of countries and people.
- Human security-less, not more vulnerability of countries and people.
- Sustainability-less, not more depletion and degradation of environment[7].

Indices of Human Development

The human development index (HDI) has been constructed every year since the very inception of human development report in 1990 in order to measure basic human development in one simple composite index and to produce a ranking of countries (Table-1). The gender related development index (GDI) and he gender empowerment measure (GEM) are composite measures reflecting gender inequality in human development (Table-2). While the GDI captures achievement in basic human development adjusted for gender inequality, the GEM (Table-3) measures gender inequality in economic and political opportunities. While HDI. measures average achievements in basic dimensions of human development, the human poverty index (HPI) (table-4) measures deprivations in those dimensions.

Human Development Index

Human development index (HDI) is a more comprehensive measure than per capita income. Income is only means to human development, not an end. HDI values range between 0 to 1 and its value shows the distance that the country has already travelled towards maximum possible value of 1 and it also shows India's comparison with other countries.

Table-I: Human Development Index

HDI rank	Life Expectancy at birth (years) 1997	Audit literacy rate (%) 1997	Combined first, second and third level gross enrolment ratio (%) 1997	Real GDP per capita (PPP$) 1997	Life expectancy index	Education index	GDP index	Human development index (HDI) value 1997	Real per capita (PPPS) rank minus HDI rank
All developing countries	64.4	71.4	59	3,240	0.66	0.67	0.58	0.637	-
Least developed countries	51.7	50.7	37	992	0.44	0.46	0.38	0.430	-
Sub-Saharan Africa	48.9	58.5	44	1,534	0.40	0.54	0.46	0.463	-
Arab States	65.1	58.6	59	4,094	0.67	0.59	0.62	0.626	-
East Asia	70.0	83.4	69	3,601	0.75	0.79	0.60	0.712	-
East Asia (excluding China)	72.8	96.1	85	14,300	0.80	0.92	0.83	0.849	-
South-East Asia and the Pacific	65.9	87.9	65	3,697	0.68	0.80	0.60	0.695	-
South Asia	62.7	53.2	52	1,803	0.63	0.52	0.48	0.544	-
(India)	**62.6**	**53.5**	**55**	**1,670**	**0.63**	**0.54**	**0.47**	**0.545**	-
South Asia (excluding India)	63.0	48.4	47	2,147	0.63	0.48	0.51	0.542	-
Latin America and the Caribbean	69.5	87.2	72	6,868	0.74	0.82	0.71	0.756	-
Eastem Europe and the CIS	68.6	98.7	76	4,243	0.73	0.91	0.63	0.754	-
Industrialized countries	77.7	98.7	92	23,741	0.88	0.96	0.91	0.919	-
World	66.7	78.0	63	6,332	0.69	0.73	0.69	0.706	-

Gender Related Development Index

The gender-related development index attempts to capture achievements in the same dimensions as the HDI-but adjusts results for gender inequality. The closer a country's GDI is to its HDI, the less gentler disparity there is in the country. But the GDI for every country is lower than its HDI, Implying that there is gender inequality in every society.

Table-2:Gender-related Development Index

HDI rank		Development index Gender-related (GDI) 1997 Rank	Value	Life expectancy at birth (years) 1997 Female	Male	Audit literacy rate (%) 1997 Female	Male	Combined first, second and third and ratio (%) 1997 Female	male	Real GDP per capita (PPP$) 1997 Female	Male	HDI rank minus GDI rank
All developing countries			0.630	66.1	63.0	62.9	80.0	55	64	2,088	4,374	-
Least developed countries			0.415	52.6	50.8	38.1	58.8	32	43	731	1,258	-
Sub-Saharan Africa			0.454	50.3	47.5	49.6	65.9	39	49	1,063	2,004	-
Arab States			0.609	67.1	64.2	46.4	70.6	54	64	1,730	6,449	-
East Asia			0.709	72.2	68.0	75.4	91.2	67	72	2,757	4398	-
East Asia (excluding China)			0.843	76.2	69.5	94.0	98.2	81	88	8,824	19,641	-
South-East Asia and the Pacific			0.692	67.9	63.9	84.4	92.2	63	66	2,605	4,794	-
South Asia			0.525	63.1	62.3	38.6	65.0	44	60	950	2,606	-
(India)	**H2**		**0.525**	**62.9**	**62.3**	**39.4**	**66.7**	**47**	**62**	**902**	**2.389**	**3**
South Asia (excluding India)			0.524	63.7	62.3	36.2	88.3	71	73	1,073	3,171	-
Latin America and the Caribbean			0.524	63.7	62.3	36.2	60.0	39	55	3,837	9,951	-
Eastem Europe and the CIS			0.752	73.7	63.8	98.4	98.8	77	74	3,314	5,226	-
Industrialized countries			0.915	80.9	74.5	98.6	98.9	93	90	17,660	30,050	-
World			0.700	68.9	64.7	71.1	84.3	60	67	4,523	8,103	-

Gender Related Development Index

Gender Empowerment Measure

The gender empowerment measure captures gender inequality in key areas of economic and political participation and decision making. It, thus focuses on women's opportunities rather than their capabilities as measured in GDI. The GEM values are lowest in Niger (0.120), Pakistan (0.176) and Togo (0.185) implying that in these societies opporturnties for women are much constrained.

Table- 3: Gender Empowerment Measure

HDI rank	Gender-related development measure (GEM) Rank	Value	Seats in parliament held by women (as % of total)	Female administrators and managers (as % of total) b	Female professional and technical workers (as % of total)	Women's real GDP per capita (PPP$)
All developing countries	-	-	10.0	-	-	2,088
Least developed countries	-	-	8.7	-	-	731
Sub-Saharan Africa	-	-	11.2	-	-	1,063
Arab States	-	-	3.7	-	.	1.730
East Asia	-	-	4.6	-	-	2,757
East Asia (excluding China)	-	-	4.5	-	-	8,824
South-East Asia and the Pacific	-	-	12.3	-	-	2,605
South Asia	-	-	6.0	-	-	950
(India)	**95**	**0.240**	**8.3**	**23**	**20.5**	**902**
South Asia (exciuding India)	-	-	5.2	-	-	1,073
Latin America and the Caribbean	-	-	15.3	-	-	3.837
EasternEuropeandtheClS	-	-	9.1	-	-	3,314
Industijalized countries	-	-	19.0	-	-	17,660
World	-	-	12.0	-	.	4,523

Human Poverty and Deprivation

Human poverty index (HPI) is a multi-dimensional measure of poverty. It is a composite index of (i) a long and healthy life (ii) knowledge (iii)economic provisioning and (iv) social inclusion. However, the dimension of deprivation are the same for both developed and developing nations. Only the measuring indices differ. For developing countries, the deprivation in a long an healthy life is measured by the percentage of people not expected to survive to age 40, deprivation in knowledge by illiteracy and deprivation in economic provisioning by percentage of people lacking access to health services and safe water, percentage of children severely underweight.

Table- 4: Human Poverty in Developing Countries; Measures

HDI rank	Human poverty index (HPI) Rank	Value (%)	People excepted to survive to age 40 (as % of total population 1997	Adult illiteracy rate (%) 1997	To safe water (%) 1990-1997	To health services (%) 1981-1997	To Sanitation (%) 1990-1997	Under weight children under age of five (%) 1990-1997	Real GDP per capita (PPP$) Poorest 20% 1980-1994	Richest 20% 1980-1994	Richest 20% to poorest 20% 1980-1994	Population Below income Poverty line % $1 a day (1985) PPP$, 1989-1994	National poverty line 1989-1994
All developing countries	-	27.7	14.6	28.4	28	-	57	31		-	-	-	-
Least developed countries	-	44.9	30.8	51.6	41	-	63	40		-	-	-	-
Sub-Saharan Africa	-	40.6	34.6	42.4	50	-	56	32		-	-	-	-
Arab States	-	32.4	13.1	41.3	18	-	29	19		-	-	-	-
East Asia	-	19.0	7.8	16.6	32	-	73	16		-	-	-	-
East Asia)excluding China)	-	-	4.7	3.9	10	-	1	-		-	-	-	-
South-East Asia and the Pacific	-	25.0	12.4	11.8	31	-	41	34		-	-	-	-
South Asia	-	36.6	16.1	47.8	18	-	64	48		-	-	-	-
(India)	59	35.9	16.1	46.5	19	25	71	53	527	2641	5.0	52.5	-
South Asia (excluding India)	-	38.6	16.1	51.6	15	-	46	39		-	-	-	-
Latin America and the Caribbean	-	14.5	9.9	12.8	22	-	29	10		-	-	-	-
Eastern Europe and the 015	-	-	8.3	-	-	-	-	-		-	-	-	-
Industrialized countries	-	-	3.1	-	-	-	-	-		-	-	-	-
World	-	-	12.5	-	-	-	-	29		-	-	-	-

GDP per capita (PPP$) rank, a negative the opposite

b. Human Development Report Office estimate.

c. Capped at 100%.

d. Heston and Summers 1999.

e. UNESCO 1997.

f. Capped at 90.0%

g. UNICEF 1999a.

h. Data refer to a year period other than the specified in the column heading, differ from the standard definition or refer to only part of the country.

i. UNICEF 1998b.

j. Human Development Report office estimate based on national sources.

k. UNESCO 1996.

l. World Bank 1997b.

m. Data refer to the latest available year.

n. The HDI ranks used this column are those recalculated for the universe of 143 countries. A positive figure indicate that the GDI rank is better than the HDI rank, a negative the opposite.

o. Human Development Report Office estimate.

p. Capped at 100%,

q. No wage data available. An estimate of 75%, the mean for all countries with wage data, was used for the Ratio of the female non-agricultural wage to the male non-agricultural wage.

r. The manufacturing age was used for the Czech Republic, Greece, Ireland and Norway.

s. The GDP per capita (PPP$) data from Heston and Summers 1999.

t. Capped at 90.0%.

u. Wage data based on Psacharopulos and Tzannators.

v. Real GDP per capita (PPP$) based on Human Development Report office estimate.

w. Data are as of 5 February.

x. Data refer to the latest available year.

y. No wage data available. An estimate of 75%, the mean for all countries with wage data, was used for the Ratio of the female non-agricultural wage to the male non-agricultural wage.

z. The manufacturing wage was used for the Czech Republic, Greece, Ireland and Norway.

aa. Real GDP per capita (PPP$) from Heston and Summers 1999.

bb. Calculated on the basis of data from UN 1994 and ILO, Yearbook of Labour Statistics 1994 and Yearbook Labour Statistics 1995.

cc. Wage data based on Psacharopouls and Tzannators.

dd. Real GDP per capita (PPP$) based on Human Development Report office estimate.

ee. Calculated on the basis of data from UN 1995 and ILO, Yearbook of Labour Statistics 1997.

ff. Data refer to the most recent year available during the period specified in the column heading.

gg. Data refer to a year of period other than that specified in the column heading, differ from the standard definition or refer to only part of country.

hh. Human Development Report Office estimate based on national sources.

ii. For the purpose of calculating the HP-!, an estimate of 25%, the un-weighted average for the 97 countries with data, was applied.

jj. UNICEF 1998b.

kk. UNICEF 1999a.

References

1. UNDP, *Human Development Report*, 1999, Oxford University Press, p.16
2. *Ibid.*, p. 16.
3. UNDP, *Human Development Report*, op. cit., p.19.
4. *Ibid.*
5. *Ibid.*p.36.
6. *lbid*, p.36.
7. *Op. cit.*

12

Good Governance: A Corporate Perspective

Brij Bhushan

To govern is to guide, is to administrate and in contemporary sense to manage. Hence governance is an art, wherein the governor takes all the means of management to govern an organisation.

In a democracy, the government is by the people, of the people and for the people. People from their respective areas, called as constituencies, send their elected leaders, who will be governing them, to the apex legislative body of our country, the parliament and the respective state legislative assemblies.

These leaders in the Parliament make the laws called as legislations to govern the people of the country and they are totally accountable to the general public, who have made them the leaders.

In the same manner, the share holders, who are the owners of these corporations elect a board of directors and who formulate the rules and regulations for the governance of the company. They are called Memorandum of Association (Largely based upon the government policies) and Articles of association, containing the internal rules and regulations of the Company.

As in a democracy the elected leaders are accountable to the public, in the same manner these governors, called as Directors are also accountable to the share holders, the employees and to the external environment of the Company.

For that matter, we can take any element of public Governance and the same is also followed in the corporate governance, like service management, performance appraisal, rewards and punishments, transparency in almost all areas of functions etc.

A corporation is a large business or company or a groups of companies, that is controlled and run together as a single organisation or entity e.g.. Reliance Industries, Tata groups of companies, Birla Groups of companies.

Corporate is relating to business corporation. It is shared by all the members of group organisation, rather than being done or possessed individually. Hence we can say that corporate is the corporate laws, corporate is the social and moral ethics followed by all the persons of the corporations etc.

Hence a good governance must have an objective, which should be based on ground realities and should be able to fulfil the expectations of public, be it the governance of general masses or the governance of a corporate.

Corporate Governance

Before we proceed further, let me give you an idea of what is corporate governance.

"Corporate Governance" is not a term which is easy to define. If I have to make you understand the same I can say that Corporate Governance is a way of life that necessitates, taking interest in every business decision. The two key elements in Corporate Governance are

(1) The enhancement of corporate performance via supervision and monitoring of management performance and

(2) Ensuring the accountability of management to share holders and other stake holders.

Corporate Governance is the system, by which corporate entities are directed and controlled.

Another important feature of good corporate governance is transparency projected through a code of good governance, which incorporates a system of checks and balances, between key players-board of management, auditors and share holders.

Hence corporate governance is a system by which corporate entities are directed and controlled.

It includes:

(1) Policies and procedures adopted by a company to achieve its objectives

(2) A code of corporate conduct and ethics in relation to all the stake holders, external or internal.

(3) Frame work of effective accountability.

Why we require Corporate Governance ?

The three main reasons for corporate Governance is

Environmental Changes

(a) Removal of trade barriers (free flow of trade in international Market).

(b) Due to enhancement of competition in the market and among the companies.

(c) Need to boost the economy.

Demographic Changes

(a) Change in employee expectation due to increase in education levels, cross border mobility.

(b) Liberalisation policies adopted by Indian Government.

(c) Global approach adopted by no. of corporate.

Corporate Failures

(a) Not keeping the pace with the environmental and fast changing demographic conditions.

(b) Not having proper supervision and monitoring of management performance and

(c) Not ensuring the accountability to all stake holders.

Therefore for all the reasons discussed, we require corporate governance.

How to achieve corporate governance ?

Now the question arises how to have corporate governance and that too an effective corporate governance. Two key issue are

1) ***Who will do ?***
2) ***How it will be done ?***

Obviously it is the corporate governors also called as **Board of Directors**, who will be governing the company, elected by shareholders.

Once again it is very difficult to have a set of guidelines for governance as it depends upon corporate to corporate but if I have to summarize the considerations required for good corporate governance then I will say that

1) To set the business performance targets and achieving them by strategic developments, according to the competitive international scene.
2) Maintaining strategic, committed and cordial relationship with the employees.

3) Having a committed, strategic and cordial relationship with the customers.
4) The use of effective technology to satisfy the customer needs.
5) Having a dynamic top management which can efficiently use and develop the people.

Let me develop upon a bit more on the role of relationship with the customer and with the employee in corporate governance. As per my personal experience I can say that if your customer is satisfied and your employee is satisfied then a major objectives of corporate governance is achieved.

For the Customer

1) It is his need that is to be satisfied.
2) The ultimate goal of all the activities in the corporation must be to satisfy the customer.
3) The 4'Ps *i.e.,* Product, Price, Place and Promotion should be for the betterment of the customer.

I remember at this instance the speech given by Mr. Bill Clinton to the members of the stock-exchange Mumbai, Where he said that the goal of all the technological advancement must be for the ultimate customer. A technology developed in America and adopted by us will not have any use if the same can not be used for the last person of our country.

For the Employees

In the same manner satisfactions of employees is also essential and in good corporate governance the following measures must be adopted to satisfy the employees

1) Sense of Identity.
2) Sense of importance.
3) Sense of development.
4) The carrot and stick Approach
5) Willingness and Motivation.
6) Good working environment.

It is said "Give it whatever it takes, get the best people and allow them to work freely, giving maximum expressions to their creativity and innovation based on a strict sense of value"

> "We must see that each person's goals are clearly defined, and he or she knows what good performance looks like. This will give them a clear focus for their energy and put them on the road to become high performing employees".

This is how in very brief I had tried to explain the good corporate governance.

Difficulties in Corporate Governance

We may face a number of difficulties while governing the corporate like.

1) Human tendency to avoid responsibility.
2) Attitudnal difference among the employees.
3) Resistance to change.
4) Notwithstanding the pace of customer frequently changing preferences.
5) Lack of top management support.
6) Discrepancies in the educational and training set up of middle and lower-level management.
7) Lack of financial resources.
8) Improper allocation of financial resources.
9) Not keeping pace with the Information Technology boom.
10) Deviance from national interest to achieve only the corporate interest.

Suggestions

1) Responsibility will be felt by the people if sense of identity, importance and development is incorporated in them.
2) Proper training and proper delegation of work with complete information to overcome the attitudinal difference among the employees.
3) To make aware the benefits after the change, which will remove the tendency of resistance to change.
4) Proper planning, including the formulation of contingent plans in changing what corporate has to give to the presently preference changing customer.
5) Maintaining the transparency, and accountability and a sense of involvement in the top management for getting their support in the corporate governance.
6) To set up the educational and training centres for middle and lower level management.
7) Having proper controlling measures not to out grow to what your financial resources do not allow.
8) Proper planning and implementations with strict controlling measures to ensure allocation of financial resources for the purpose they are meant for.

9) Taking advantages of technical advancement, specifically in information sector, to have the state of the art technological developments in the corporations.

10) The corporation must keep their national interest ahead of the corporate interest for the long term existence and development of the corporation.

Conclusion

No corporate can be effectively governed unless a balance between management techniques and the accountability of the organisations to the various stake holders is not maintained and hence a corporate governance which is built upon trust, transparency and accountability can be regarded as a good one and the most effective one.

The goal of good corporate governance must be to build star performs, who can attract the best of minds to join the organisation and to create a strong sense of ownership in them. Ownership is not just offering stock options, it has more to do with an emotional engagement and integration with the organisation.

13

Alternate Framework of Governance

M. M. Sankhdher

The production of Nuclear bombs by indigenous technology, rejection of Security Council resolution as illegal and arbitrary, refusal to accept outside mediation on Kashmir, insistence to solve mutual problems with Pakistan bilaterally, snubbing U.S.A. for meddling, showing guts not to be cowed down by P5 or G8 economic sanctions, asserting claim for nuclear weapons state status and taking strong security on the borders as well as tightening internal security against insurgency, proxy war and infiltration and launching a diplomatic offensive to protect national interests and demanding permanent membership of the UN Security Council- these are open indicators of the Swadeshi wave sweeping across this country. Welcoming global investments for economic and industrial growth but not allowing multinationals to dominate our economy or capture neo-colonial markets are encouraging signs of the emergence of a strong Swadeshi movement engulfing the country.

The same Swadeshi spirit seems to have impelled the Government to initiate a process of constitutional review.

The inclusion of the item, "Review of the Constitution" in the National Agenda of the BJP Alliance Government followed by Prime Minister Atal Bihari Vajpayee's announcement during the debate on the confidence motion in the Parliament generated a public discussion, not so much on the provisions which need to be relooked but on the propriety or otherwise of undertaking the exercise of revising some parts or the whole of the Constitution. The attention has thus been misdirected to non-issues to the neglect of the substance of the question involved.

To say that the Constitution after 50 years of age needs to be reviewed does not imply any blasphemy or disrespect of the document, which has served a useful purpose during a crucial period after independence. Review does not mean violating any sacredness that it has gathered during the course of its functioning as a framework of governance. The very fact that it has been amended 79 times alone shows that it cannot be treated as a religious scripture. Those who argue the reverse unnecessarily suspect malafide on the part the party in power as if it is going to throw away the "basic" principles or structure to the wind. It is unfair to read such an intention in the innocuous official statements, even when the names of likely distinguished members of the proposed Constitution Commission have not been announced.

Leave aside the narrow political-partisan angle to view the question, there is need to consider it objectively and dispassionately, disallowing polemics, platitudes or gimmicks to intrude in this vital debate in all seriousness. In an open, democratic society, even extreme views, of asking for a new Constitution should not be condemned or brushed aside. May be review of the Constitution throw up ideas for a thorough overhaul of the statute without overhaul of the statute without meaning any disrespect to the enormous labour put in the Constituent Assembly at some historical juncture. It is quite possible for researchers to come across certain outdated, irrelevant features. Which could be replaced by new provisions which the constitutional pundits might be able to formulate, giving the Constitution great usefulness and longer sustainability.

On the face of it, there is no harm in undertaking the onerous task of a positive review of the Constitution on the threshold of the 21st Century, now that the nation is marching towards self assertion self-awareness and self identity as never before. The country is facing unprecedented challenges social, economic, moral, global and political. We need to examine whether the given Constitution and the structures it has produced would be able to cope with the rising crescendo of demands and people's aspirations for a better, more evolved life of human beings now surviving at a bare level of animal existence. Whether the present Constitution will enthuse the classes and masses for designing and achieving higher goals than the mundane goals of daily existence? Whether the Constitution reflects the national the glorious cultural heritage and the time-tested traditional values which alone can inspire self confidence and national esteem so much needed to take the country forward to the enviable position that Bharat deserves among the community of the nations?

The present Constitution is a valuable instrument for scrutiny of the merits and drawbacks of our political system-a political system comprising functions, processes, structures and organised institutional relationships. Reexamining the political framework, provisions and guidelines would, inevitably, bring in its train the whole package of problems associated and affecting our collective national life. Both constitutional legal orthodoxy and socio-economic radicalism will fall into a pattern of national evaluation. In the fast changing world of today, India cannot afford to remain tied down to a model received 50 years ago, when circumstances and problems were of a totally different character. An ancient country with a lot to contribute to human evolution of the modern world is not supposed to follow dogmatically a pattern of ideas and practices largely initiated from the west. Let us realize to what extent the present Constitution system hamstrung our progress and also its capacity to renew and renovate the national psyche by the inherent spiritual resources that our society so proudly commands. Whether or not, the Constitution helps in the recovery of the national prestige we have lost in recent centuries at the hands of invaders and colonisers? In what way can we reckon the successes and the failures of the Constitution in the establishment of democracy, federalism, social justice, harmony, freedom and what we have ?

The concept of Swadeshi, when applied to the making of a Constitution as a framework for good governance postulates a guiding spirit of nationalism/patriotism where the governing principle is the love of the motherland. Political management should breathe this spiritual sentiment in policy formulation and governmental action. The prompting of national ideology should inform political reflection and field performance. The Indian Constitution perhaps only assumes this spirit; this spirit is not explicit or exhibited in the language or phraseology of the provisions. A reviewed Constitution may remove this serious lapse in order tint a common citizen feels enthused to respect it as his own. Presently, the lawyers, politicians and judges, by and large, seem to be more drawn towards it. Even the voter, the bedrock of the political system, hardly ever glances into it, not to say gets inspired by it.

The intellectual elite need to look into the Constitution from the point of view of satisfying the Swadeshi criterion. The persisting alienation of the citizen from the Constitution can be removed by integrating him spiritually with the supreme political code. This is not the occasion to spell out the detail, of the Swadeshi proposition, but a few basic formulations may be put forward. The details can be worked out later when more comprehensive review of the Constitution is taken.

First, now is the most opportune time to attend to this problem because luckily the tune for Swadeshi is the loudest event. There are compelling reasons for this new consciousness in the ruling class: internal insecurity external dangers, neo-colonialism of the multi-nationals, U.S. tendency to monopolise nuclear arsenals and a desire to police the whole world as a single Super-Power and threats from neighbours, notably China and Pakistan. Besides anti-national forces, spying agencies, infiltration's and insurgencies, have awakened the nation from its slumber in the interest of national self preservation. Objective factors propel review of the predicament where the country has to gird up its loins to face the critical situations staring directly into our face. A sober realization has downed on the rulers and the ruler make amends in thinking and behaving impinging on the imperative of maintaining national sovereignty, dignity and honour. Swadeshi in foreign. Swadeshi in economic progress and Swadeshi in Constitution and Polity are the dominant watchwords of the current phase of political discourse.

While the popular trend is towards accepting Swadeshi as the national creed, the English educated urban elite would strongly react to denouncing as national chauvinism, jingoism and fascism. How to convince those who refuse to be convinced? Their eyebrows are raised and they come out with a signature campaign condemning Swadeshi.

The Swadeshi concept is to treat power as service by motivating the ruling class to lead an austere life, dedicated to serve national interest selflessly. The Constitution should search some checks and balances for inculcating Swadeshi in the rich class for investing in indigenous industry and work as trustees of the welfare of the working class. Imbibing Swadeshi virtue in the rural feudal class would imply a change in character towards fraternity, compassion, social service and religious harmony. The chapters on Fundamental Rights and Directive Principles should be rewritten towards this end. Our Functioning democracy, which has developed numerous evils of party behaviour and electoral malpractices, wastage in administration, the criminal and politicians nexus and unscrupulous power game through use of vote banks, cheap populism, etc. needs radical reform of the constitutional system. A Swadeshi pattern of democracy can be ingeneously evolved.

Appendix

Action Plan for an Effective and Responsive Government*

Introduction

The Government, both at the Centre and the State, share the concern for ensuring responsive, accountable, transparent, decentralised and people-friendly administration at all levels. There is, however, considerable frustration and dissatisfaction amongst the people, especially the weaker sections of society, about the apathy, irresponsiveness and lack of accountability of public servants, even as the expenditure on staff continues to increase. There is increasing anxiety about growing instances of corruption and criminalisation in public life and administration. The people, particularly the vulnerable, groups, are also greatly concerned about the deterioration in the performance of agencies concerned with law and order and the investigation of offences. Their faith in the registration of offences, their timely investigation and the delivery of prompt justice has been eroded.

Time has come for a strong message to be conveyed that administration is for the people and not for the public servants themselves. There has to be a change of attitudes, and public servants should realise that efficiency will be measured not in terms of what the services purport to offer, but in terms of public satisfaction. Simultaneously, there has also to be a cleansing of the services and codification of the ethics, value systems and the interface with the politicians.

Necessary corrective steps must be taken to arrest the present drift in Government and public services, and take urgent measures to restore the faith of the people in the fairness and capacity of administration. With this objective, the Prime Minister had inaugurated a Conference of Chief Secretaries in November, 1996 on 'An Agenda for an Effective and

---

* IJPA, New Delhi; July-September, 1998.

Responsive Administration'. In the Conference, a number of issues were raised which emphasised the need for bringing about a transformation in the public services to make them more efficient, clean, accountable and citizen-friendly. The conclusions of the Conference, which were sent to the State Governments for implementation, are given in Annexure I.

Following the Conference, a national debate has been generated throughout the country to elicit views from a wide crosssection of people. Responses have been received from retreats organised in Mussoorie and Hyderabad, and a number of leading academic institutions in Delhi and other places. Written communications have been received from officials, experts, voluntary agencies, citizens groups, media, etc. Follow up action has been initiated on some of the priority areas to demonstrate the determination of the Government of India for implementing these reforms and to provide models for adoption by the State Governments.

The focus of these discussions has been to evolve a concrete Action Plan, for gearing up the Government machinery to provide a responsive, transperent and clean administration to the people and to address issues of reform and morale in the civil services. The Action Plan proposed to be discussed in the Conference includes initiatives in the following areas:

1. Making administration accountable and citizen-friendly,
2. Ensuring transparency and the right to information, and
3. Taking measures to cleanse and motivate Civil Services.

The adoption and implementation of the proposed Action Plan for an effective responsive administration would require a strong political will, and reiteration from both the Central and the State Governments of their commitment to provide an accountable and responsive administration. Instances of responsive administration and initiatives taken by the central and State Governments already are described in the supplementary notes given in Annexure XI.

Accountable and Citizen-Friendly Government

The citizen's perception of the State and its functionaries is primarily based on its role as a service provider, law enforcer and regulator. Improving the quality of administration and provinding a responsive interface between the citizen and the public services require initiatives in following areas:

1. Citizens' Charter

The State Governments and the Ministeries/Departments at the Centre are all involved in some manner or the other, in providing public services. Apart from an overall lack of transparency and accountability in the System, most delivery systems suffer from ad hocism and delaly. It is.

therefore, important to identify and publicise the standards of services and time-limits that the public can reasonably expect, particularly in critical activities with a public interface. Government of India has directed Ministers/Department and other agencies with public interface to formulate a Citizens' Charter, lay down time-limits and standards for services, avenues of grievance redressal, and put in place monitoring systems and independent scrutiny to sure implementation of the Charter. A number of Departments have already formulated such Charters. Though the Charter is not proposed to be made justiciable, it would carry a moral commitment of the Government and would provide a framework under which public services can be evaluated. The principles of the Citizen' Charter have been enunciated at Annexure II which the State Governments can use to formulate their own charter according to their needs. Some model Citizens' Charters are given in Annexure II for information.

2. Redressal of Public Grievances

The poor record of most public agencies in the area of prompt and effective redressal of public grievances is a major cause of public dissatisfaction and a subject of criticism by the elected representatives. Public grievances primarily arise out of the inaccessibility of officials, failure to even acknowledge applications, non-enforcement of any kind of time-limits, and unsympathetic attitude of officials at various levels. A note highlighting the areas of action is given in Annexure III to enable Central and State Governments to review their existing system of redressal of public grievances, and institute measures not only for streamlining these, but also to monitor the steps taken to improve their efficacy.

3. Decentralisation and Devolution of Powers

Responsive Government would also require complete decentralization of delivery of services through fully empowered elected local Government bodies, both in rural and urban areas, consistent with the spirit of the 73rd and 74th Constitutional Amendments. The Central/State Government need to take steps to strengthen the financial and administrative capacity of the local bodies and vest them with adequate respources and powers. A note on the subject is given in Annexure IV.

4. Review of Laws, Regulations and Procedures

In the changing administrative scenario, particularly in the context of economic liberalisation a number of existing laws and regulations have lost their relevance. The laws and regulations militating against the interest of the weaker sections of the society and the poor are required to be urgently amended. Similarly, existing procedures also need to be changed to make the whole process of approvals, sanctions, etc., simpler and transparent. Government of India has initiated a comprehensive exercise for amending the Civil procedure Code, Company law and a number of other laws, as well as to reduce the time taken in disposal of cases in civil and criminal courts. It is necessary the State Governments undertake similar exercises in this regard and effect necessary changes in the laws and regulations. A note on the need to review existing laws, regulations and procedures is given in Annexure V.

Transparemcy and Right to Information

It has been noticed that secrecy and lack of openness in transactions in responsible for corruption in official dealings, apart from being contrary to the spirit of an accountable and democratic Government. Consequently, there is a demand for introducing greater transperency in the functioning of Government departments and public bodies. There is also a need to ensure to the people an easy access to all information relating to Government operations and Government decisions, as well as that on the performance of the Government, except to the extent specifically excluded by raw. It is increasingly realised that, more the effort at secreacy, the greater the chances of abuse of authority by the public functionaries. Therefore, the following two areas/issues need to be addressed in this regard

1. Transparency in Government and Right to Information

There is a widespread consensus on the need to assure freedom of information to the public and to amend such laws that stipulate unnecessary restructions on free access of the public to information. Government decisions need not be clouded in secrecy, except in the interest of national security. Based on the discussion of an Inter-Ministerial Working Group, a ststutory scheme to ensure freedom of information subject to certain safeguards, and to amend a number of central legislations, has been formulated. Details of these are given in the Annexure VI. State Governments could undertake a similar legal exercise, while endorsing the Central initiative, and ensure greater openness in the working of the Government departmnets, public agencies and elected local bodies, and provide information on procedures for various statutory approvals.

2. Access to Information

It is also important to improve the access of the public to information from public offices, through streamlining of internal procedures, computerisation, and by setting up public facilitation counters in offices. It is proposed that all the offices under the Government of India and the Public Sector undertakings will have computerised facilitation/information counter so that information and assistances is available to the public on various essential services and approvals. The State Governments may consider setting up of similar facilitation counters not only at the municipal and district levels, but also in the various State Directorates. A note on the subject is given in Annexure VII.

Improving the Performance of the Public Services

The civil services in India have played a significant, indeed a critical, role in maintaining the integrity of the country and in bringing about major developments in post-independent India. However, in recent times, the services have been facing a grave crisis of identity and role definition. People now believe that public services are meant to benifit government servants and politicians and not the public. The emphasis here is on all publics services which subsume all technical, professional law enforcement and administrative personnel. Though issues relating to efficiency and effectiveness of the administrative machinery have been discussed from time to time, the reforms initiated have only dealt with minor procedural changes, without really addressing the issue of improvement in the quality of services, The Government had initiated an exercise to discuss the specific reforms that could be undertaken to improve the image of the services and enhance their effectiveness. The following proposals ad emerged in this regard:

1. Code of Ethics

Adoption of the Code of Ethics of public services based on Constitutional principles and values, with appropriate amendments in the existing codes of conduct. Such a code, given in Annexure VIII, not only seeks to regulate the role of the civil servants, but also specifies the relationship between employees in public services and politicians, so that the basic commitment of the civil servants towards the welfare of the public and the principles enshrined in the Constitution is reiterated.

2. Cleansing the Administration

Though the rationale for the civil service in promoting the progress and integrity of the country is as valid today as before, thee is an urgent need to tackle corruption and the increasing erosion of moral values in public life. The recommendations which have emerged in this regard have been collated in the note given in Annexure IX. These, measures, once adopted, would need to be widely publicised to instil public confidence, both in the probity of all political and administrative functionaries, and In prosecution of the corrupt without exception.

3. Stability of Tenures and Constitution of Civil Services Board

Frequent and arbitrary transfers of public servants affect the ability of the system to deliver services effectively to the people. It has been seen that implementation of area development programmes and poverty alleviation schemes suffer where the officials are shifted frequently. Since the success of such schemes depends on having officials with sufficient local knowledge and understanding to execute the schemes. Hence, it is felt that arbitrary transfers really operate against the interest of the people. In this context, the note given in Annexure X propose a schemes for State Governments to constitute high-powered Civil Services Boards to decide on transfers and postings of senior officials, on the same lines as the one already followed by Civil Services Board at the Centre.

Future Action

The above-mentioned package of measures, proposed as a part of the Actions Plan on a responsive and accountable administration, would include both a number of one-time actions for immediate consideration, such as the Freedom of Information Act, Citizens Charter, measures to tackle corruption and grievances redressal; as well as long term and ongoing reforms, such as inculcation of ethical values, objective criteria for transfers and placements, judicial and legal reforms, computerisation, building employees morale and orientation of public functionaries. However, there can be little doubt that any Action Plan is only as good and credible as its level of implementation and monitoring. It is proposed that the Plan itself can be elaborated and operationalised in concrete terms, and then pursued individually by the Central. and State Governments. The progress, under various items of Action plan, would continuously be monitored by the Cabinet Secretary in close consultation with the Chief Secretaries of the various States and Union territories. The Action Plan would need to be well publicised, not only to secure widespread acceptance and feedback from all the stakeholders, but also to enlist the cooperation of the people in the implementation of the plan and in its evaluation.

Action Plan

1. Citizens' Charter and an accountable administration,
2. Effective and speedy public grievance redressal system,
3. Empowering elected local bodies in rural and urban areas and decentralised delivery of services,
4. Review of laws, regulations and procedures,
5. Transparency and Right to Information,
6. Access of the public to information from public offices and creation of facilitation counters,
7. Code of Ethics for public services,
8. Tackling corruption and cleansing the administration, and
9. Stability of tenure and a scheme for Civil Services Boards.

Annexure I

Operative Recommendations of the Conference of Chief Secretaries

The Recommendations of the Conference grouped under three headings: (1) responsive administration, (2) cleansing civil services, and (3) commitment to principles in the Constitution are given in the following paras.

Responsive Administration

1. The crisis in administration calls for a redefinition of the role of government and its function and its real focus to serve the public effectively as much as to ensure efficient and cost-effective administration. Accountability, transparency and cleansing public service are all interconnected issues for ensuring a clean and responsive administration. It is necessary to converge the efforts of various public agencies for delivery of basic services in rural and urban areas and for single-level dealings with the public. This calls for steps to reorganize work procedures, for delegation down the line and an effective management information system accessible to all. Simultaneous steps to address the right-sizing of public services, value for money on public expenditure, restoring, effective audit, monitoring and evaluation, good financial management systems, etc., are needed.

2. It is necessary to introduce greater transparency and openness in the functioning of Government and public bodies. This would cover, for example, movement towards a Right to Information Act, Transparent and well-publicised procedures for approvals by the general public and entrepreneurs under various statutes and regulations for: allotment of land and immovable property; systems of assessment, levy and collection of various taxes and charges; award of work tenders for construction and provision of Services; procurement of goods and services; and various arrangements for involvement of private sector in contracting of services; and infrastructure projects by suitable amendment of relevant laws. The aim should be to move towards a citizen-centred administration.

3. The citizens in urban and rural areas should be provided with widespread and easy access-through the media, posters and various forms of neighbourhood-level communications-to all in formation relating to Government operations and reverse the undue emphasis on secrecy, details of various Government and local schemes, information on award of tenders and procurement, procedures for identification of beneficiaries under various Government schemes, and for receipt of benefits thereunder, publication of scores for all cases of admission to colleges and for recruitment, delivery of various

civil services, etc. The progressive computerisation of information on public operations and work procedures will be of benefit to the government and the people.

4. Accountability should be interpreted in a larger sense in relation to public satisfaction and responsive delivery of services. We may consider the phased introduction of Citizens' Charter for as many service institutions as possible by way of citizens' entitlement to public services, collaboration of consumer organisations and citizen groups-wide publicity to standards of performance, quality, timeliness, cost, etc., for public services, and the provision for periodic and independent scrutiny of performance of the agencies as per set standards.
5. Immediate measures are needed for strengthening the machinery for grievance redressal at all levels, increased thrust on the needs of disadvantaged and vulnerable sections, attention to systemic reforms, meaningful efforts to reach the unserved public-spirited citizen panels to assess service organisations, gender sensitive approach at all levels, and well-understood systems of filing complaints relating to poor services and malfeasance and prompt action thereon, accompanied by close monitoring of delays and punishment of the delinquent while devising ways to filter frivolous complaints. The good examples in different states should be widey publicised and scaled up along with due recognition for innovation and citizen-friendly attitudes.
6. The fullest possible decentralisation of service delivery and the administration of income support schemes, and effective utilisation of available resources, through the elected urban and rural local bodies, accompanied by the required devolution of powers and resources.
7. Encouragement to the widest possible awareness and participation of citizens and various representative groups in local decision-making, and the implementation of schemes affecting their livelihood and quality of life.The media has an important role to play in this regard.
8. Urgent steps for legal reform, for access of the citizens to quick and cheap justice, while initiating steps for amendment and simplification of the concern laws and obsolete legislations for introducing simple and speedy procedures. A number of laws and regulations militating against the interest of the poor need to be quickly amended.

Cleansing the Civil Service

1. It is recognised that responsive administration depends on reforms in civil service at all levels, adherence to ethical standards, and basic principles of the Constitution, and a clear understanding of the relationship regulating the civil servants and the politicians. It has to

be clearly appreciated that the political executive should concentrate on policy formulation while implementation is left to public services at various levels.

2. The approach to eliminate corruption in public service needs to address prevention, surveillance and deterrent prosecution, and deal ruthlessly with the nexus between criminals and unscrupulous elements. It requires concerted efforts of politicians, public services and all stakeholders in civil society. The existing procedures for departmental enquiries and vigilance proceeding should be revamped. Rules and legal provisions should be amended to enable immediate and exemplary prosecution and removal of corrupt officers without giving them recourse to any political protection. It is necessary to remove the scope for any interference in the prompt prosecution and punishment of corrupt officials. It is necessary to devise systems to break the nexus between politicians, bureaucrats and criminals which has developed in a number of places.
3. The numerous service and conduct rules should be reviewed in order to arrange for the review of the integrity and efficiency of officers at any stage during the career, and the compulsory retirement of officers of doubtful integrity.
4. Simultaneous with the measures given above, the preventive steps would include not only regulatory reforms to reduce scope for discretion and secrecy at all levels, developmental schemes and approvals.
5. Other in-built steps should include improvement in service conditions and right-sizing public services, improving the system of performance appraisal and promotions through transparent procedures, recognised systems of rewards and penalties, consistent action of senior management to support the subordinates in sincere performance of duty according to law and procedures, and in resisting illegal directions. Equal attention is needed to review recruitment procedures, training at induction and subsequent levels, and development of personnel at the operating levels.

Commitment to Principles of the Constitution

1. The Government of India and State Governments should draw up a Charter of Ethics and Civil Service Code for the civil service, based on fundamental principles of the Indian Constitution such as secularism, equality, impartiality, social justice, attention to the needs of the Weaker sections, rule of law, etc. This code would regulate the role of the legislators and the relationship between civil servants and politicians.

2. It should be agreed that the loyalty of public servants should be only to the service for the public and the rule of law. This is particularly relevant in the context of the permanent character of civil service.
3. State Governments will be requested to devise suitable mechanisms, including a high-powered Civil Service Board, and amend relevant rules for transparent decisions on postings, promotions and transfers of senior officials on the lines of Central Government. Similar Boards should be set up to govern functionaries at lower levels and in elected local bodies. These boards could be strengthened in their apolitical functioning by the appointment of Civil Services Ombudsman to deal with grievances of officials. It should be recognised that the public suffer equally from frequent transfers of heads of departments. Appropriate legislations may be considered to incorporate some of these suggestions.

Annexure II

Citizen's Charter and Accountable Administration

SCHEME

One of the important means of ensuring accountability and transparency in the agencies engaged in providing services to the people, or enforcing laws and regulations, is to organize their actions around the concept of Citizens' Charter. This part of a national movement in countries, like the UK and Malaysia, where it lays out the citizen's entitlement to public services and responsive administration of regulations. It places the citizen at the centre of administration instead of making him a passive recipient of services rendered indifferently with no concern for quality, timeliness or cost. It is to be seen as a visible symbol of accountable government. The Government of India has directed all Ministries, Departments, and agencies under them, with a public interface to publish Citizens' Charter, starting with services. The object is to bring all the service rendered by these agencies under the charter over a period of two years.

Citizens' Charter is based on the principles of: (1) wide publicity of standards of performance of public agencies and local bodies; (2) assured quality of service; (3) access to information and courtesy and helpfulness of staff; (4) choice and consultation with the citizens; (5) simplified and convenient procedure for receipt and acknowledgement of complaints, and time-bound redressal of grievences; and (6) the provision for independent scrutiny of performance with the involvement of citizen groups.

While it is not justiciable, it represents the moral and democratic commitment of the government to service of the public.

In order to accomplish this task, it has been directed that each Central Government Department and its public agencies should work out its own Citizens' Charter and related actions in terms of the nature of work and, more importantly, the groups of clients or members of the public, geographical concept, nature of regulatory function and paid-for services. It should also evolve a plan containing both long-term and short-term/ moving targets for improved public satisfaction and efficient performance through systems improvement, technological and information inputs, staff orientation, work place changes, use of alternate providers, partnership with citizen groups, voluntary agencies and the corporate sector, etc. An in-built machinery will be set up in each Ministry/Department for independent system auditing and periodic monitoring of performance with reference to the Charter principles and to attend to the capacity building and orientation of the staff. It is envisaged that consumer organisations, citizen groups, experts, retired public servants, elected representatives and others are involved in this process of formulation and scrutiny of performance so as to ensure that the commitments made actually meet the needs of the people. Once the areas of activities sought to be improved are streamlined, adequate publicity will be given so that the people are made aware of the proposed changes. The entire process will be monitored periodically by a core group under the Cabinet Secretary.

Many Central agencies, such as the Railways, Post, Health, Central Board of Direct Taxes, Central Board of Excise and Customs, Petroleum, Industry, Delhi Development Authority and Passport Office and others have announced a series of citizen-friendly initiatives. The Ministry of Home Affairs have set up a Task Force to formulate specific steps for a citizen-friendly law enforcement system and crime prevention. It has also announced setting up of a Police Complaints Authority for Delhi. The Central Health Ministry has requested all the State Governments to set up emergency care services in bigger hospitals on the pattern of what has been considered for Delhi, as also a system of registration and rating of nursing homes. State Governments, like Himachal Pradesh, have announced a Citizens' Charter for revenue functionaries.

Proposed Action

The State Governments could consider formulation of Citizens' Charter on the lines indicated above of services provided by various State and local agencies with public interface, such as the Offices of the Collector, Superintendent of Police, Municipal bodies, Zilla Panchayat, Tehsil and Block Office, Transport Department, electricity offices, water supply and sanitation services, etc. Monitoring systems similar to those proposed in Government India could be installed to ensure availability of sustained benefits to citizens. The concept of the model office based on computerised counter services will be an important means of implementing the Charter. The close association of citizen groups, elected representatives and media could be considered for success of the venture, and for continuous feedback on performance through independent citizens' panels.

Annexure III

Effective and Speedy Public Grievance Redressal System

The poor record of most public agencies in the area of prompt and effective redressal of public grievances is a major cause ot public dissatisfaction, and the subject of criticism by elected representatives. It is noticed that many of the Government Departments and their subordinate offices, which have substantial public interface/ and where large numbers of public are required to go daily, do not display the required orientation to the needs and circumstances of the public, especially the weaker section of society, women and the handicapped.

It is also found that adequate facilities are often not available in the public offices for reception of the public seeking various types of information or with various queries and demands of services, and arrangements for seating and waiting of the public, water supply and sanitation, protection from rain, sun, etc., are insufficient or non-existent in police stations and other public offices which the citizens are required to Visit. There are often no display boards relating to information generally desired by the public on the location of offices and facilities, various procedures involved, fees, submission of forms, time taken in disposal, etc. The names of grievance redressal officers are not often widely published, and these officers are also not accessible as stipulated to meet the public.

Apart from lack of facilities and friendly reception, the public grievances primarily arise out of inaccessibility of officials, failure to even acknowledge applications, unwarranted delays and non-enforcement of time limits, lack of information, harassment and activities of middlemen, demand for speed money, ignorance of procedures and forms, and the unsympathetic attitudes of officials at all levels. In big cities, citizens are often required to travel long distances to visit different offices due to lack of decentralised locations at the ward level for providing information on dealing with complaints. The methods for payments of various taxes and service charges are often inconvenient, not suited to the working hours of such members of the public who do not have access to servants. As regards the villagers in dispersed villages throughout the district, they face great problems in approaching the tehsil and district offices for getting copies of records, licenses, payments, applications under various Government schemes, etc.

State Governments have instituted systems of time-bound redressal of citizens' grievances, which are often monitored through computers and programmes like Administration to the People in Andhra Pradesh. The district officials are required in many States, like Tripura to visit villages and blocks together periodically in order to listen to the grievances of the people, and redress them on the spot Janta Darbars are also convened by Ministers.

The progress in respect of disposal of public grievances is being monitored in the Central Government by the Department of Administrative Reforms and Public Grievances. The Directorate of Public Grievances in the Cabinet Secretariat deals with cases of individual grievances for Central agencies with a large public interface, and has the power to call officials and the concerned files to give a binding order. Central Ministries like Railways, Posts and Telecommunications have set up Lok Adalats to deal with complaints in the presence of the consumers. There are social audit panels of imminent citizens which look into the quality of services of the Postal and Telecommunications Department. There is an Ombudsman for the commercial banks. The Central Manual of Office Procedure provides for the fixation of time limits for dealing with public grievances, while the Code of Conduct Rules provide for disciplinary action in case of discourteous behaviour or negligence in grievance redressal.

Similar arrangements can be considered at the state level. Apart from cells located in the office of Chief Ministers, as in fact is being done in states like Tamil Nadu, Karnataka and Haryana. This will help in high-level attention to systemic causes of grievances through delegation, decentralisation, flexible norms, simplified procedures, review of forms, etc. The performance review of officials could incorporate attention to grievance redressal and public perception of the services of the agency.

A number of measures could be considered for immediate improvement in the situation. The language and tone of various application forms should be user-friendly, and the forms be widely available in various outlets, including post offices. Every office should display at a prominent place its organisational structure, indicating names of officers and their functions, and location of their rooms. Every public servant should normally be available during working hours to respond to the public in person or on phone. Every application or petition should be acknowledged through standards acknowledgement slips. Every application should also carry such a slip for future response. Time-limits should be fixed for approval or rejection of applications for permits, quotas, certificates and approvals, on the basis of well-publicise and uniformly applied critieria. This should be accompanied by delegation of financial and administrative powers at the operational, level and well-enforced standards of accountability. The District Administration should set up mechanisms to contact the people at the local level periodically, specially for remote and inaccessible areas. Senior officials, like Collector and Superintendent of Police, should not get so overloaded with work or committees that they are unable to devote enough time to meet people regularly and deal with their problems.

The number and periodicity of contact for the people with Government offices would be minimised, and the officers should allow for the flexible needs of the working population. Every department should choose a few priority areas from the citizen's new point for computerisation and allow free access of the citizens to this information in this computer. Finally, every public body should have a well-defined mission statement spelling out standards of service provided to the public, such as garbage removal, water supply to power supply. The officials responsible for good work should be given recognition and reward, and the innovative practices should be widely disseminated.

The real issue, however, is the need to bring about a total change in the attitude of public servants towards redressal of public grievances at all levels and to pin-point responsibility for action on grievance of the people. This is dependent internally on measures to improve their levels of motivation and morale through rewards for good work and punishment for deliberate negligence and through awards for suggestions. The senior officers should constantly supervise the staff at the cutting edge level in policestations, sub-division, etc. Every official in public offices should wear name badge.

A demonstrable and effective way of ensuring prompt redressal of public grievances would be through establishment of independent Public Grievances Committees, consisting of eminent citizens. Such Committees can be authorised to inspect the adequacy and functioning of grievance redressal systems in various public offices, and report to the Cabinet Secretary (for Central Government) and Chief Secretary of State Government, on actions to remedy the system, and to take firm steps against negligent officials. It is also possible to set up independent watch dog committees at district level to report to State Government on the working of grievance redressal systems. The Himachal Pradesh Specific corrupt Practices Act makes the omission on the Part of an officer to discharge his statutory or bone fide duty a corrupt practice. Similar enactments or the provisions of draft Karnataka Administrative Procedure Bill could be considered to oblige officials to respond to requests of the public.

Proposed Action

The State Government could consider an urgent review of the system of redressal of public grievances at the State, district, city, block and village levels, and devise arrangements for their sensitive and prompt redressal, and ensure regular independent review of these systems. Steps could be taken to fix responsibility in each office for dealing with grievances, for attitudional orientation of officials at all levels, and for continuous monitoring of the redressal system. This could be integrated with the overall package of measures for responsive administration. The State Government could consider dettong upindependent watchdog committees at the district and city levels to report to high-powered cells in the State Government on the functioning of the local grievance redressal systems, as well as cases of negligence and delay.

Annexure IV

Empowering Elected Local Bodies in Rural and Urban Areas and Decentralised decentralised Delivery of Service

CONTEXT

Responsive administration requires that service delivery and administration of income support schemes are decentralised through the elected local bodies in rural urban areas. This alone makes for meaningful democracy, as atriculate in the 73rd and 74th Constitutional Amendments. These Amendments contain the provisions for regular elections, constituting District Planning Committees, drawing up illustrative list of functions, and establishment of State Finance Commission for assigning commensurate resources to local bodies. The Central and State Governments envisage implementation of all the poverty alleviation schemes and integrated rural development through the panchayats and nagarpalikas. States like Kerala and Andhra Pradesh have made a success of bottom-up planning by providing the help of resource persons to enable Gram Sabhas to prioritise their needs and prepare development plants. Examples abound of support to the widest possible participation of people, women and NGOs in the planning and delivery of services, which also eliminates the delay and costs of bureaucratic intermediation.

At the same time, the agenda of real empowerment of elected local bodies, has largely not gone beyond conforming legislation in most States. Centralised system for Planning and service delivery often through functional agencies, still persist, and the local self-government bodies and the elected functionaries are not enabled to function with adequate control over local functions and resources, The functions for each tier of Panchayati Raj need to be demarcated and commensurate resources vided on the basis of recommendations of State Finance Commission.

The transfer of local function to the elected local bodies will also help in the right-sizing of State Governments, pervaded the former are giving adequate personnel and administrative support. The constitution of District Planning Committees to prepare plans for economic development and social justice, as already done by Kerals, will help to consolidate village and city level plans, based on local priorities and people's contribution. The NDC has already recommended that 41 per cent of the plan resources be set apart for decentralised planning.

The Panchayati Raj Institutions and the Nagarpalikas would also provide an umbrella for the convergence of various sectoral, poverty alleviation and area development programmes at each tier, including schemes focused on women, disadvantaged groups, children, etc. Their involvement in the selection of beneficiaries for various welfare and income support schemes would help to cut down corruption and leakages in these schemes. Madhya Pradesh and Rajasthan provide examples of the benefits of transparency in public distribution system, development works, public hearing, etc., with the oversight of Panchayat bodies and local volunteers. As the Approach Paper for the Ninth Plan asserts social audit and transparency in the functioning of Panchayati Raj Institutions is crucial for their growth.

Proposed Action

The Central and State Governments could move purposefully to ensure the effective empowerment of elected local bodies in urban and rural areas, as envisaged in the 73rd and 74th Amendments, through the assignment of all local functions and planning according to the illustrative Lists in the Constitution, accompanied by steps to strengthen their implementation and financial capacity, and the vesting of executive powers in these bodies. The State Government could also take early steps to devolve adequate resources, commensurate with the assigned tasks and decentralised delivery of services, based on the recommendations of State Finance Commissions. The central and State Governments could encourage and sustain untary agencies and people's participation in all the schemes for the delivery of basic services identified in the Conference of Chief Ministers in July, 1996 and in all local development schemes. All village-level schemes could be reoriented and integrated under the Panchayati Raj, and bottom up participatory planning could be encouraged. Cooperatives and similar self-governing systems could be encouraged in all spheres of economy and resource management.

Annexure V

Review of Laws, Regulations and Procedures

Background

In the course of review of the experience with implementation of various policy changes announced by the Government in the context of economic reform and liberalisation of procedures for inflow of foreign investment, it has been found that foreign investors and small and big industrialists alike cite administrative red tape, requirement of multiple approvals, and cumbersome rules and regulations causes of delays and cost escalation, and less than commensurate benefits flowing from policy initiatives of the Government. The effective delivery of services and benefits under various welfare schemes to the public are also frustrated by rigid procedures and archaic laws, apart from insensitive attitude of the officials and unwarranted transaction costs.

It has pointed out that many of the old laws, rules, regulations and procedures in the Central and State Governments have lost their relevance considerably. Many of them not only stand in the way of a responsive administration, but are found to be often operating against the interest of the poor and the marganialised groups. Laws on the subject operated by one or more departments often overlap or conflict with each other, leading to fruitless parallel proceedings. They also increase the cost of transactions and litigation tremendously for the average citizen and subject him to corruption at every stage. The opaqua regulations, however, allow the unscrupulous builders and middleman to break the rules with impunity, sometimes in collusion with the officials.

It is recognised that various State Governments have undertaken detailed exercises to simplify and liberalise various rules and regulations. Many Central Ministries have also been addressing the issue seriously and a major exercise for amending various laws affecting economic reform, industries and urban development is under way. The Law Ministry has taken up an exercise for legal reform, having regard to the recommendation of expert committees, to reduce the time taken for disposal of cases in courts, to provide for alternate systems of dispute resolution, to reduce the scope for unnecessary adjournments, facilitate pre-trial conciliation, etc. The Finance Minister has also announced a series of legal initiatives and review of present laws in the Budget speech.

Central and State Governments could review the regulatory and legal framework in different economic and social sectors to see whether the objectives for which the regulations were put in place are properly defined, after consultation with affected groups, whether these objectives could be better achieved in any other manner or made more citizen-friendly, whether it is necessary to continue the existing regulations at are, whether the machinery for their implementation is adequate and cost effective and whether the presumed social and economic benefits of the regulations warrant their continuance. Where there are a number of orders of government on the subject, every Department should bring out a comprehensive government order on the subject every five years. It should also bring out lists of Acts and Regulations implemented by it every five years, along with informative notes in the local language for wide dissemination.

The review of by the States, in turn, could cover the multiplicity of forms and return, and the design of the forms itself, as well as the possibility of making transactions paper-less, as have been tried out by the Central Excise Department in Delhi. It should be possible to receive the applications to various agencies required from an investor or the applicant at one point and help him to secure the clearance of all the agencies. The number of required clearances could be cut down, and the process of approval itself can based much more on self-regulation. Building commencement certificates would be issued by architects, and various certificates could be issued by accredited persons or agencies with severe penalties on the issuing persons for any violation.

Some of the suggested requirements for effective decision making included:

1. Reduction in number of levels and stages (including calling for a number of certificates) through which decision-making process goes through, so that the Government progressively reposes more faith in the citizens in matters like issue of licences.
2. Delegation of financial powers should be in relation to the current price levels and should be reviewed every three years.
3. It is necessary to review the present provisions of audit and place more emphasis on systems audit to reduce enormous delays due to fear of audit even in trivial matters, disproportionate to the expenditure involved.
4. All public officers should publish handouts in simple local language, the procedures to be followed, the method of filling forms, fees and other requirements, and make them available to the public on demand.

It is possible for the Central and State Governments to work together in this important exercise since it is the essence of more citizen-friendly administration, access to swift justice, reduced corruption, and success of the economic reform process. It will also help to effect savings in the huge time, manpower, and legal costs incurred by central and state Governments, and their agencies, in pursuing litigation without any hope of a final result for many years.

Proposed Action

The central and State Governments could draw upon agenda for priority reform of the legal system and procedures to facilitate economic reform, reduce obstacles to economic and social activity of the poor and marginalised groups, to enable speedy flow of services to target groups in various schemes, to facilitate early approvals under various states, to provide the people access to swift and inexpensive justice, and to cut down the tendency of cases in criminal and civil courts. A core group of central and state officials and legal experts could be set up to review efforts already taken/under way in this regard, and suggest area of legal and regulatory amendment/reform to the next meeting of the Chief Minister after wide consultation. Meanwhile, the Central and State Governments could proceed expeditiously with amendments to restrictive laws and procedures, where the proposals are finalised.

Annexure VI

Transparency and Right to Information

CONTEXT

There is a political consensus and popular demand for introduction of greater transparency in the functioning of government and public bodies, and widespread and easy access of people to all information relating to Government operations and Government decisions, as well as performance of the Government, except to the extent specifically excluded by law. A new culture of information and helpful attitude, as opposed to secrecy and mystification, should pervade all government offices.

It is increasingly realised that, more the effort at secrecy, the greater the chances of abuse of authority by the public functionaries. At the same time, the provisions of Official Secrets Act, 1923, and the Code of Conduct Rules for Government employees prevent most of the information about affairs of Government from being disclosed to the public. The most damaging consequence of the legislation and the Code of Conduct is the generally secretive behaviour which it has encouraged in the civil service, and the denial of items of unclassified information, and the details of development expenditure, to the citizens. The Budget speech of the Chief Minister, Tamil Nadu, mentions that one major reason for occurrence of irregularities is that information leading to decision taken by the officers at various levels do not reach the public.

There have been efforts since 1990 to introduce legislation to ensure Freedom of Information, and to amend the Official Secrets Act. The call for greater transparency and Right to information has been given in a number of States. Some States have issued circulars to ensure the availability to the people of details of development expenditure and inspection of revenue records in public offices, apart from the provision for public hearing. Chief Minister, Andhra Pradesh has announced that a White Paper will soon be issued on giving Information to the people. Bilaspur, in Madhya Pradesh, is implementing a transparent public distribution system and recruitment for jobs. The budget speech of the Chief Minister, Tamil Nadu, refers to the proposal of the State Government to enact a law to provide the public Right to Information. According to the Chief Minister, this will enable the public to get details about the schemes of the Government, the works executed by various Departments, the essential commodities supplied to each of the shops under Public Distribution System and pave the way for the people to question the irregularities in the system.

The Government of India set up a working group under the Chairmanship of Shri H. D. Shourie to formulate a Bill for Freedom of Information, and amendments to relevant laws for this purpose. Based on the discussions of this Group, a statutory scheme has been formulated to ensure freedom of information subject to certain safeguards in public interest These are outlined in the Appendix at the end of this Annexure.

Amendments to other Enactments and Rules

Simultaneous with the proposals for enactment of the Freedom of Information bill, the Government of India is also formulating amendments to Section 5 to the official Secrets Act, and Sections 123, 124 and 125 of the Indian Evidence Act to bring them in line with the provisions of the new legislation. It is also proposed to amend the relevant sections of the Central Code of Conduct Rules in order to enable Government employees to release information to the public consistent with the provisions of the new legislation. The rules relating to classification of official documents ınd records are also proposed to be amended suitably.

A detailed exercise could be carried out by an Expert Group to identify various Central and State Laws which contain provisions relating to release of information, and propose amendments to bring them in line with the Freedom of Information Act. Pending action to pass these legislations, detailed instructions could be issued to all the Central Ministeries/ Departments, and agencies and PSUs under them, to introduce greater transparency in their operations, and to ensure widespread and easy access of the public to all unclassified information. This can be followed up by department, specific instructions to be issued and enforced by each department.

Proposed Action

The Central and State Governments could endorse immediate formulation of the legislation for freedom of Information on the lines of the statutory scheme, amendments to the relevant provisions of the Official Secrets Act, 1923 and the Indian Evidence Act and other relevant laws. They could process consequential changes in Code of Conduct Rules, Classification of official records, etc. The legislation for Freedom of Information may be introduced in Parliament at the earliest. The administrative arrangements for its implementation may be worked out in three months by a group of Central and State officials and legal experts to be constituted by the government of India.

In the meantime, the Central and State Government could issue instructions for greater openness in the working of Government departments, public agencies and elected local bodies, and providing information widely on procedures for various statutory approvals, details of allotment of land and property, criteria for assessment and levy of taxes, criteria for, and information on, award of work tenders and procurement of goods and services, criteria for and selected lists of, beneficiaries under various Government schemes, building approvals, development expenditure on works, etc. Counters could be set up in public offices for easy and prompt availability of such information to the public. The employees at all levels could be oriented and directed to be courteous and open in dealing with the public and in the provision of information not prohibited by law.

Appendix

A Statutory Scheme for Freedom of Information

PURPOSE

The statute may be called Freedom of Information Act. It may be enacted by Parliament and shall come into force from a date to be notified in the Gazette. Its purpose would be to progressively provide greater access to information under the control of Government of India, State Government, Union Territories and other governmental agencies and organisations substaintially controlled or funded by the Government (hereafter referred to as public authorities), in order: (a) to promote openness and transparency in administration; (b) to enable fuller and more meaningful participation of the people in making and implementation of policies and programmes affecting the public; and (c) to promote accountability and responsibility in administration.

To fulfil these purposes, the right of access to information would be provided to citizens on the broad principles that: (a) access to information should be the rule and denial of access the exception; (b) the grounds for denial may be clearly and specifically defined; and (c) there should be a provision for an independent mechanism which provides remedy to applicants against decisions to withhold information.

Scope

The scheme should apply to all Ministries/Departments of Central/ State Governments and their attached and subordinate offices and other bodies, including PSUs and autonomous bodies, substantially funded or controlled by the Government and local bodies excepting bodies/ organisations, such as intelligence services, that may be specifically exempted from it. So far as the judiciary, Tribunals and such other judicial/ quasi-judicial bodies and Parliament/State Legislatures are concerned the scheme would only cover their administrative/support services with the concurrence of the Chief Justice or the Speaker, as the case may be.

Obligations on Public Authorities

Each public authority should publish periodically, and keep updated information indicating: (1) particulars of its organisation, functions and responsibilities; (2) description of its decision making processes in terms of procedures and powers and responsibilities of its officers and employees; (3) Norms for performance of activities such as prescribed periods for their processing and completion, physical and financial targets, etc., and the actual achievement with reference to such norm; (4) Classes of records under its control, including the rules, regulations, instructions and lists of manuals, etc., used by its employees for carrying out activities; (5) The facilities provided for access to information; and (6) The name, designation and other relevant particulars of the officer, to be called the Public Information Officer, to whom request for information may be addressed.

It shall also be the duty of the concerned officers of a public authority to give reasons for decisions-whether administrative or adjudicative-to those affected and to disclose the relevant facts and analyses when major policies or decisions are announced.

Grounds for Refusal of Access in Certain Cases

Access to information may be refused where:

1. The request is too general or of such a nature, that having regard to the volume of information required to be retrieved or processed for fulfilling it, it would involve disproportionate diversion of the resources of a public authority or would adversely interfere with normal functioning of such authority; provided that, where access is being' refused on the ground that the request is too general, it would be the duty of the Public Information Officer in a public authority, to help the

requester as far as possible to reframe his request in such a manner as would facilitate compliance with it;

2. The request relates to information that is required by law or convention to be published at a particular time; and
3. The request relates to information which is already contained in published material available for sale.

Procedure and forms of Access

Each public authority shall appoint officers to be called Public Information officers in its offices, who should be vested with adequate administrative authority to obtain relevant information within their Qrganisations. While appointing these officers, the public authority concerned shall keep in mind the overriding need to provide access to information as conveniently, cheaply and effectively and as close as possible to a citizen's place of residence or business.

It will be the responsibility of the Public Information Officers to deal with requests for access to information and to ensure timely compliance with such requests where the information being requested for is not being withheld or access is not being refused. The decision whether to accede to requests or not would also be taken by him.

A request under this Scheme should be made in writing and should, as clearly as possible, specify the particulars of the document or record to which access is being sought. Where a citizen cannot, for a valid reason, make a request in writing, the Public Information Officer may either accept an oral request or assist the requester in making a written request.

The Public Information officer shall endeavour to provide access as expeditiously as possible and a decision in the matter should be taken within the maximum period of 30 days from the date of receipt of the request. In case the decision is to refuse access, the grounds for refusal should be clearly indicated, along with a description of the review procedure open to the requester.

In the event it is not possible to respond to a request within the period of 30 days, the period may be extended up to a maximum of another 30 days for reasons to be recorded and communicated to the requester, in writing.

Lack of response from a public authority, within the above mentioned period, shall be deemed to amount to a refusal of request for access to information and the requester shall be entitled to seek recourse to the review procedure.

Access may be provided in one or more of the following forms: (1) A reasonable opportunity to inspect records/documents; (2) Supply of copies of documents; or (3) Where the information requested for is stored in computers, a provision of access through terminals or supply of print-outs, etc.

Access should ordinarily be provided in the form it is requested for unless: (1) it would disproportionately divert the resources of a public authority; or (2) would be detrimental to safety or preservation of the record document in question.

Fee

Fees may be charged for access to information and may include an application fee and an additional fee based on the cost of supplying the information, such as cost of research involved in compiling the information and cost of copying, etc. The fee may be waived in the cases where the disclosure can be said to be in the larger public interest.

Exemptions from Disclosure

Disclosure of information may be refused if the information is covered by any of the following categories:

1. Information disclosure of which would prejudicially affect the sovereignty and integrity of India, security of the State, conduct of international relations, including information received in confidence from foreign governments, their agencies or international organisation;
2. Information disclosure of which would prejudicially affect the conduct of Centre-State relations, including information received in confidences from a State Government or any of its authorities/agencies;
3. Information in the nature of Cabinet papers, including papers prepared for submission to Cabinet or submitted to Cabinet, other than the documents whereby such decision are published;
4. Information, other than exclusively factual information, in the nature of internal working papers, such as inter-departmental/intra-departmental notes and correspondence, papers containing advice, opinion, or recommendation for the purpose of deliberative processes in a public authority;
5. Information, disclosure of which would prejudically affect the enforcement of any law, including detection, prevention, investigation or suppression of crime or contravention of any law; or would lead to incitement to an offence; or would prejudicially affect the operations of any intelligence organisation to be specified by the Government, or would prejudicially affect public safety or the safety of an individual; or would prejudicially affect fair trial or adjudication of a pending case; or would reveal the existence or identify of a confidential record

or source of information, or would prejudice future supply of information relating to violation in or contravention of any law;

6. Information the disclosure of which would prejudicially affect the Government's ability to manage the economy or would prejudicially affect the legitimate economic and commercial interest of the public authority, or would cause unfair gain or loss to any individual or organisation;
7. Information, the disclosure of which would prejudicially affect the management of services under, and operations of public authorities.
8. Information in the nature of trade or commercial secrets or any information having a commercial value, which is likely to prejudicially affect the competitive position of a third party provided that, excepting in the case of trade or commercial secrets protected by law, disclosure maybe allowed public interest in such disclosure, outweighs in importance any possible harm or injury to the interest of any such third party;
9. Information, the disclosure of which would not subserve any public interest;
10. Information, the disclosure of which would cause unwarranted invasion of the privileges of an individual; and
11. Information, the disclosure of which may result in the breach of Parliamentary privileges or would amount to violation of an order of a Competent Court

Severability

If a request for access to information is refused on the ground that it is in relation to information which is exempted from disclosure, then notwithstanding anything contained in this Act, access may be given to the part of the document which does not contain any information that is exempted from disclosure under this Act and which can reasonably be severed from any part that contains any such information.

Third Party Intervention

Where a public authority intends to disclose information has been supplied in confidence by a third party, or which might contain trade or commercial secrets of a third party, and such disclosure can reasonably be expected to harm the interest of such third party, a notice may be given to it of the intended disclosure and it may be permitted to make a representation within 14 days of the receipt of the above notice, stating reasons why the information should not be disclosed. The public authority shall take such representation into account while taking a decision on the request for information. In the case of information other than trade or commercial secrets protected by law, disclosure may be permitted if public interest ouweighs in importance any possible harm or injury to the interest of the third party.

Internal Review

A requester, whose request for access to information has been rejected by an Information Facilitation Officer, may make an application for review of that decision, to the Head of Department having jurisdiction over the concerned office of the public authority to which the request had been addressed.

The review application shall be disposed of by the concerned Head of Department within 30 days of its receipt. In case the request relates to information in the nature of third party information, the disclosure of which can reasonably expected to cause harm to such third party, the Head of Department shall also send an appropriate notice to such third party affording it the opportunity to make a representation, and shall take into consideration any such representation, if made, while taking a final decision on the review application; provided that, excepting in case of trade or commercial secrets protected by law, disclosure may be permitted if public interest outweighs the expected harm or injury to the interests to any such third party.

A review application may also be made as regards the fee proposed to be charged by the Information Facilitation Officer.

Appeal

The Machinery under the Consumer Protection Act, 1986 may be used as an apellate mechanism with an appeal under the Freedom of Information Act being dealt within the same manner as a complaint under the Consumer Protection Act.

Rules and Regulations

Rules and regulations may be made to carry out the purposes of the Act. They may deal with matters, such as fees and waiver of fees, forms of application for access, reyiew and appeals against dicisions to deny access, procedures for review, appeal and other similar matters.

Annual Reports of Public Authorities

All public authorities shall, in their annual reports, include a separate chapter detailing the operation of the Act. The reports may mention, inter alia, statistical data including the number of requests for access to information received during the year, the number of refusals along with broad reasons for refusals, the costs incurred in providing access and the fees recovered, details of review applications and appeals and their disposal, etc.

Council for Freedom of Information

Councils may be set up at National as well as State levels, under the chairmanship of the Ministers in charge of Department of Administrative Reforms with a suitable number of members representing such interests as may be specified, for reviewing the operation of the Act and to advise the Government on making the Act effective, including training and orientation of employees, streamlining procedures, etc.

Review of Other Laws and Rules/Regulations

There are a number of laws containing provisions which may impinge on disclosure of information which would need to be reviewed and amended to make them consistent with the proposed Freedom of Information Act. For example, the vision of Sections 5 of the Official Secrets Act will have to be amended suitably, keeping in view the principles underlying the proposed Freedom of Information Act. Similarly, Sections 123, 124 and 125 of Indian Evidence Act may need to be reviewed. Rule II of the Central Civil Services (Conduct) Rules, 1964, and its corresponding provision, *i.e.,* Rule 9 of the All-India Services (Conduct) Rules, 1968 would also need to be amended. Similar action would need to be taken in respect of the relevant rules for the State Civil Services. The Working Group on Right to Information and promotion of open and transparent government is looking into some of these aspects. However, a detailed study is required to identify all laws which may have to be revised.

Annexure VII

Computerised Access of the People to Information from Public Offices and Facilitation Counters

SCHEME

An integral aspect of administrative reforms, both in the short term and in the longer perspective, is related to the speedy and easy access of information to the public on the services and activities of Government and the development of appropriate Management Informations Systems in Government. There are considerable delays in redressal of grievances and securing access to information, since government department with a public service interface do not have a mechanism to provided information to the citizens across the counter or to deal with their queries and complaints at a single point.

This would necessarily involve two areas. The first is related to the development of an appropriate computerised network of information to internally link all offices of Central Government, Telecom or Railways, as well as to integrate Central or State offices for effective information sharing in the cause of services to investors and the public, and more intelligent government. The second aspect would be linked to the need to ensure widespread and easy access of citizens to information at various levels in the Government, and its agencies, as well as the issue of revenue records and certificates, simplified and speedy systems of securing approvals and permits, redressal of grievances, etc., with the help of computers.

The Expert Group set-up by the Government of India is examining these issues. Meanwhile, the Government is studying the legislative amendments or new laws necessary to ensure the legal and transactional acceptability of computerised data transfer and print outs.

It is evident that a significant infrastructure to create a computerised public interface is already available through National Informatics Centre (NIC), which is working closely with the state governments. The district NICNETs are fully operational, and district level NIC coordination Committees have been setup to supplement the Committees at the State Level. NIC has already setup 6,000 data bases and the GISTNIC is providing information on various aspects of the economy and functioning of Government, to which a new section on public services is now proposed to be added. All the districts are proposed to be computerised with NIC help over the next few years, to provide up-to-date information on judgements and the stage of cases, with 150 courts covered already. Many state governments are taking full advantage of the facilities provided by NIC, including the Central Assistance for the computerisation of land records, and have also devised their on systems to computrise procedure information to public, etc. States like Andhra Pradesh are monitoring the movement of files, and implementation of schemes through computers.

As part of the programme to disseminate information on public services to the public, it is proposed to set up citizen information centres on a pilot basis (starting with all State Capitals) through the efforts of the Department of Consumer Affairs and Public Distribution, and the involvement of state governments. These centres would be run by voluntary agencies with assistance from the Consumer Welfare Fund. However, the real help needed by the citizens in terms of securing various services or getting their complaints promptly attended to, besides information on procedures and forms, can be provided only through counters set up in public offices.

The Government of India has decided that all officers of the Government and agencies under it should have a computerise public interface, aimed at dissemination of information to the public for a fee or free of charge. The Central Government Ministries and their agencies would take steps to ensure provision of all unclassified information on procedures and decisions to the public through facilitation counters which should be set up near the reception hall of the Ministries or offices, similar to the Lakhina model in Maharashtra. These counters would be operated continuously during the day by trained officials with courteous approach, with the capacity to converse in English and the local language, and capable of using computers. The salient features of the facilitation centre are given at the end of this annexure. These counters can be provided with computer consoles to provide instant information on the status of pending cases, waiting lists, etc., and also print out permits and licences across the counter wherever possible.

The State Governance could consider similar steps to identify services most frequently required by the people, and set up people facilitation counters in all offices with a public interface in the districts and towns, State Departments, Directorate and Public Utilities. The Central Government could consider supporting the establishment of these counters through help from the NIC training of staff, etc., and ensure delegation of powers and procedural changes for this purpose. The Central and State Governments can jointly work towards providing the people of India in all tehsils, districts and towns so that, over the Ninth Plan period, all the public offices have at least one information and facilitaion outlet for the harassed consumers or the applicant. The facility could be extended to the police stations at the same time.

Proposed Action

The State Governments could consider steps to promote widespread and easy access of the people in rural and urban areas to information on public services, details of Government schemes, status of applications, allotments and permits, etc. They could ensure this through a systematic and phased computerisation of administrative operations with the help of NIC, and the emphasis on providing quick information and assistance to the people across the counter for priority services in all offices with public interface. This could be linked with the scheme for public facilitation counters in all government offices.

Appendix

Public Facilitation Centre: Salient Features

- Provide-information regarding services, schemes and procedures through brochures, booklets, reports, etc.
- Provide information regarding position of waiting list and applications through computer, screens updated every day, and through computerised query to departmental data base.
- Provide information regarding matters, such as bill payment, registration, land/house allotment, payments, etc., or phone or personally to the public.

- Forms which are to be utilised for various procedures should be available at the Facilitation Centre, even if the processing is to be done elsewhere.
- Receive complaints, issue acknowledgement slips, indication the section dealing with the complaints.
- A sufficiently senior officer is to man the Facilitation Centres with appropriate orientation, capable of speaking English and local language for handling customers, and knowledge of use of computers.
- Time limits and other details be notified through display boards at the Faciliation Centres for completion of various procedures and for disposal of cases.
- Ensure easy accessibility to Facilitation Centres for the customer and average citizen, and publicity regarding the location and hours of access.
- Utilising Interactive Voice System where feasible for enquiry response.
- Benches and fans for the waiting public, especially the old and the handicapped.

Annexue VIII

Code of Ethics for Public Service

Responsive and clean administration depends, interalia, on adherence of the employees in public services to ethical standards and the basic principles of the Constitution, such as secularism, social justice, attention to the needs of weaker sections and vulnerable groups, equality and rule of law.

Both Central and State Governments no doubt have notified regulations governing the conduct of employees in various services which address these issues. However, they are more in the nature of formulations of do's and don'ts, and do not represent a positive statement of values and beliefs that should govern the public and private conduct of civil servants.

Nor do they provide clear directions to the employees on certain issues effecting their morals, motivation, sensitivity, and professional skills. This is relevant at the present juncture, when there is much confusion regarding the desirable service norms for these services, and the rewards from adherence to the highest standards of probity and integrity. There has been support for such a code from both officials and members of the public.

It is in this context that the enclosed Code of Ethics has been formulated. It spells out the employee's obligation to the Government and the Constitution, the right of public comment, conflict of interest, accountability to the public, concern for the value of public assets, release of information, integrative role, professionalism, and teamwork. It clearly brings out the expected behaviour of the employee in case of illegal directions of superiors, the need to refrain than seeking favour from politicians, the principles of responsive administration, supportive role of senior officers, and the role of public services in a secular Constitution wedded to the Rule of Law and Directive Principles of Policy. The Code would apply to all services, generalist and technical. The Government of India proposes to give a legal shape to this code by incorporation it in the Code of Conduct Rules for the All India Services and Central Government employees.

Proposed Action

This initiative of the Central Government for assuring values in the public services could be endorsed by the State Government and they could consider enforcing the Code of Ethics as an integral part of the Code of Conduct Regulations for State Services, after appropriate changes to suit local circumstances.

Appendix

Code of Ethics for the Public Services in India

OBJECTIVE

The objective of Code is to prescribe standards of integrity and conduct that are to apply in the public services. The principles stated below underlie and supplement the rules and laws regulation the public and private conduct of various public services.

Obligation to Government and the Constitution

The Constitutional and administrative role of the Public services is to assist the duly constituted Government, of whatever political colour, in formulating and implementing policies of the Government and in administering the public services under the Central of the Government in the most effective and efficient manner, within the framework of the Indian Constitution.

It is the obligation of every employee in the public services to uphold the Rule of Law and respect for human rights, and to act solely in the public interest while making recommendations or exercising administrative authority. He or she must maintain the highest standards of probity and integrity.

In relation to the general public, employees in the public services should conduct themselves in such a manner that the public feels that the decisions taken or the recommendations made by them are objective and transparent, and are not calculated to promote improper gains for the political party in power, for themselves or for any third party.

Employees in the public services should not seek to frustrate or undermine the policies, decisions and actions taken in the public interest by a duly constituted Government, be declining or abstaining from action which flows from ministerial decision or statutory obligations. Where, following the instruction of the superior authority implementation of such decisions or action would appear to conflict with the exercise of impartial professional judgement, or affect the efficient administration of the department or undertaking, the employee should set out the points of disagreement clearly and courteously in writing to the superior authority, and seek explicit written instruction thereon.

Where an employee in public services has reasonable grounds to believe that he or she is being required by the superior authority to act in a manner which is illegal or against prescribed rules and regulations, or if any legal infringement comes to his or her notice, he or she should decline to implement the instruction. He or she would also have a right to bring the facts to the notice of the Head of Department or the Chief Secretary (Cabinet Secretary in the Central Government) or the Minister. It shall be incumbent on the Chief Secretary (Cabinet Secretary in the case of Central Government) to examine the issue carefully and advise the Chief Minister) Prime Minister in the case of Central Government) appropriately.

Right of Public Comment

Generally, employees in public services have the same rights of free speech and independence in the conduct of their private affairs as other members of the public. However, they also have a duty not to compromise the Government by public criticism of, or comment on, policies. They should, therefore, ensure that their contribution to any public debate or discussion on such matters maintains the discretion appropriate to the position they hold, and is compatible with the need to maintain a politically neutral Public Service.

Conflict of Interest and Peer Pressure

Employees in public services should refrain from decision in respect of which they have reason to believe that they are calculated to benefit any particular person or party at the expense of the public interest.

Every employee in the public services shall disclose any clash of interest when there is conflict between public interest and private interest, or he or she is likely to benefit from any act of omission or commission while discharging his or her functions.

Employees in public services should be alert to any actual or potential conflict of interest, financial or otherwise, and should disclose this to their superiors, whether the conflict covers them or their family members.

Employees in public services should maintain their independence, dignity and impartiality by not approaching politicians and outsiders in respect of service matters or private benefit, and exercise peer pressure to dissuade those within their own cadre who do so, and to set in motion disciplinary proceedings against such persons. Any such approach on his or her behalf in such matters would be deemed to be at the instance of the employee.

Accountability and Responsiveness to the Public

Consistent with accountability to the superior officers and the Ministers in accordance with Constitutional provisions, employees in the public services should be accessible to the people and practice accountability to them in terms of quality of service, timeliness, courtesy, people orientation, and readiness to encourage participation of, and from partnerships with, citizen groups, for responsive Government.

Employees in the public services should be consistent, equitable and honest in their treatment of the members of the public, with particular care for the weaker sections of society, and should not ever be, or appear to be, unfair or discriminatory. Decisions in pursuit of discretionary powers should be justifiable on the basis of non-arbitrary and objective criteria.

Employees in the public services should accept the obligation to recognise and enforce the citizen's right for speedy redressal of grievances and commit themselves to provide service of declared quality and standards to the citizens.

Employees in public services should respect the right of the public to information on all Government activities and transactions except where they are debarred from releasing information by provisions of law or valid instructions.

Concern for Value of Public Assets and Funds

Employees in public services should avoid wastage and extravagance, ensure effective and efficient use of public money within their control, and endeavour that the benefits of schemes for disadvantaged and poor sections of society are not wasted or diverted for the benefit of others. They should avoid ostentation and set examples of austerity for others.

Non-Abuse of Official Position

Since employees in public services have a responsibility to take decisions on merits, and they are in a position of trust, they must not use their official position to influence any person to enter into financial or other arrangements with them, or with anyone else. They must not abuse official position to obtain a benefit for themselves or for someone else, in finanacial or other forms.

Safeguards in Release of Information

Employees in the public services should not unauthorisedly release information which is not permitted by law, or compromise private or business interests, or the privacy of an individual when such information has been received in confidence. They should not take improper advantage of official information acquired in the course of their work, for unwarranted gain themselves or others.

Integrative Role

Every employee in public services should recognise the integrative role of public services in national development, and resist internal and external attempts to fragment public services and society on caste, communal or religious lines. He or she should cultivate national outlook to rise above sectarian, service, cadre or departmental loyalties.

Continuous Improvement Through Professionalism and Teamwork

It shall be the duty of every employee in the public services to continuously upgrade his or her skills and knowledge, strive for creativity and innovation and nurture values of team working and harmony.

All employees in public services should promote and exhibit public and private conduct in keeping with the appropriate behaviour and standards of excellence and integrity. They should support the juniors in the latter's efforts to resist wrong or illegal directives and in abiding by the Code of Ethics. At the same time, they should reward good work and punish any dereliction of duty or obligations, based on objective and transparent criteria.

Annexure IX

Tackling Corruption and Cleansing Administration

The Context and Consequence

It is not an exaggeration to talk about corruption in terms of a crisis or a cancer endangering India's society, polity and economy. There has been a distinct increase in transactions in Central and State Governments, where the presence of corruption has been substantiated. Evidence points to an increase of corruption in higher bureaucracy and elected political functionaries, often in collusion or in nexus with criminal elements. Corruption is rampant in administration of welfare schemes, public distribution system, police, revenue and irrigation departments, and several other sectors where people come into contact daily with administration. Corruption at lower levels takes the form of speed money for expediting approvals or providing legitimate services, or bribes for twisting rules. A matter of grave concern is the vertical integration of corruption at various levels of government between officials and politicians and the inability of top functionaries to check the prevalence and growth if corruption. Corruption in public life is of course part of the malaise of black money and erosion of the moral fibre of Indian Society.

The effect of corruption on the economy and public administration in terms of waste, distorted resource allocation, reduced revenues, unfavourable perceptions of foreign investors, etc., is obvious. More insidious from the point of view of responsive government and the welfare of the poor, is diluted standards of goods, services and construction, hazards to life and safety of the public from spurious goods, leakage of benefits and subsidies meant for the poor and the denial of fair treatment and justice to people other than those able to access money and influence. That is why there is a strong demand by the public for effective punitive and corrective measures to tackle the problem. This concern is reflected in the manifestoes of all political parties in the 1996 General Election.

The Scheme

The Government of India is committed to integrity and impartiality in public life and clean administration, and to take effective steps to eradicate the evil of corruption. It is determined to pass the legislation for Lok Pal in the current Session of Parliament. Along with similar statutory steps by the States, it should be possible to proceed vigorously in cases of allegations against ministers and public functionaries through an independent institution with credibility and assured powers.

Along with this following steps can be considered for investigation and prosecuting quickly all cases of corruption and misconduct of officials at all levels and for ensuring swift and exemplary punishment of the guilty:

1. Elimination of corruption in public services should address preventive, surveillance and deterrent punishment, and deal ruthlessly with the nexus of officials with criminal elements and venal political functionaries.
2. Rules and legal provision should be amended to enable immediate and exemplary prosecution and removal of corrupt officials without recourse to any political protection.
3. There should be no scope in the rules for any interference in prompt prosecution and punishment of corrupt public servants, and permission for such prosecution should be given within a prescribed period to investigating agencies, like the CBI, where prior approval has been stipulated. At the same time clear norms should be laid down to prevent demoralisation of public servants on account of frivolous complaints or inquiries.

4. The Investigating agencies and vigilance machinery should be strengthened by provision of adequate staff, powers, resources and independence, accompanied by proper accountability for results. The Preventive aspect of corruption in government or the public sector depends on an independent and well-staffed vigilance set-up.
5. Amendments should be formulated to the relevant rules on the lines of those proposed in the rules relating to All India and Central services to provide for the premature retirement of officials at a reasonably early stage of employees' careers to weed out elements which are either inefficient or of doubtful integrity. It is further necessary to amend the relevant Service Rules to enable the review of integrity and efficiency of officials at any stage during their career, and to provide for premature retirement of officers of doubtful integrity in public interest.
6. The existing procedures for departmental enquiries and vigilance proceedings for Central and State Government employees should be revamped in order to ensure their completion within a year. The proposed steps in Central Government include:

(a) Prescribing firm time limits for all the stages from preliminary investigation to issue of chargesheet, to actual enquiry and the issue of final orders of exoneration or punishment;

(b) Ensuring, through training, compliance with all legal requirements of enquiry and opportunity to the defendant so as to avoid procedural infirmities that lead to legal challenge;

(c) Agreeing with Public Service Commission and Chief Vigilance Commissioner on time limits for consultation and advice;

(d) Ensuring adequate number of full-time or part-time inquiry officers, and providing them with adequate incentive and training;

(e) Suspending or transferring to non-sensitive posts those personnel who are being prosecuted or proceeded against departmentally on charges of corruption;

(f) Providing for summary procedures in cases where charges relate to penalties other than removal, dismissal and reduction in rank;

(g) Dealing with deficiencies pointed out by the Courts of Law; and

(h) Making a careful distinction between petty procedural irregularities and substantive misconduct to eliminate the former from detailed inquiries and close such case after recording adverse remarks in the CR, issue of warning or counselling the officer.

7. Attachment and forfeiture of properties (movable or immovable) acquired by public servants by corrupt or illegal means not only in

their own names but also in the names of their relatives and others under their control can be considered, through provision modelled on the Smugglers and Foreign Exchange Manipulators (Forfeiture of Property Act, 1976); and prompt penal action in respect of proven holding of assets disproportionate to known sources of income.

8. Areas of discretion available to various levels of administration should be curtailed to the minimum, along with steps to prevent their arbitrary use. Equally urgent are steps for deregulation, procedural simplification, elimination of unnecessary controls, decentralisation and delegation, monitoring of service delivery through citizen groups, greater transparency in all areas of public interface and corruption prove agencies, and the review of the rules and procedures governing procurements, contracts and extortion, as these would bring down the incidence of speed money on the one hand d extrusions at the decision-making level.
9. Objective and transparent criteria for the transfer and promotion of officials in order to insulate them from political influence in action taken according to law and in public interest.
10. Strengthening role and powers of Audit in the identification of financial and procedural irregularities to be followed by investigation for possible corruption.
11. Close networking of different agencies like Lokpal/Lok Ayukta, CBI/CVO, Income Tax authorities, Enforcement Directorate and CAG in terms of sharing of information and intelligence, and coordinated investigations.
12. Encouraging adoption of code of Ethics not only by civil servants but also all public functionaries, media, professionals, and the corporate sector based on constitutional principles and moral values.
13. Assuring adequate remuneration, congenial working conditions and access to housing and health care for the employees.
14. Mobilising public opinion against corruption, increasing awareness avenues of complains and investigation, and supporting efforts of citizen groups, media and NGOs in this respect..
15. Encouraging officials at all levels to bring irregularities or suspected corruption to the notice of the Chief Secretary, and to reward such officials in cases where the fraud reported by them are established.

Points for Decision

The Central and State Governments could draw up, adopt and implement measures suggested above consistently and effectively, with an agenda of long and short-term actions, and based on total coordination of Central and State agencies and the CAG. The Lok Ayuktas could be adequately empowered and resourced to deal effectively with all cases or allegation of corruption. The efforts could be centred on immediate and exemplary prosecution and removal of corrupt officials without any political protection, while supporting honest and competent employees. The agenda could be monitored regularly by the Prime Minister/Chief Minister, Cabinet Secretary, Chief Secretary and the results would be widely publicised so as to instil public confidence in the probity of all political and administrative functionaries.

Annxure X

Stability of Tenure and a Scheme for Civil Services Boards

Background

It is not sufficiently realised that the effective and people-friendly administration of various policies and schemes of the Government, and the responsive delivery of services, depend critically on the stability of tenure of senior officials incharge of the programmes, and enforcement of laws. The responsiveness of a civil servant, and his capacity for evenhanded treatment of all sections of the public, depends to a subtantial extent, on the degree to which he or she has a sense of continuity in the official position and does not feel threatened by the risk of premature transfer or any punishment for even-handed administration. The effectiveness of public administration in the States suffers from the ease with which tenures of officials serving in the field either in the regulatory or development field are cut short, leaving the officials demoralised, the public dissatisfied, and with the credibility of the Government seriously eroded. The public in fact perceives such actions as reflective of an unholy nexus between undesirable elements among politicians and civil servants. To impart stability to tenures of officers at the cutting edge of field administration, like District Magistrates, Superintendents of Police, Heads of Departments, etc., would not only help the officers to deepen their knowledge and experience, but also help the public to receive the services expected of the civil services with expedition and efficiency. The consequences of irrational and abrupt transfers are manifold. Most importantly, they result in unstable, short tenures, leading to frustration and demoralisation; the 'partiality' and 'objectivity' of the officer comes under strain; building up of experience-based expertise is prevented; and ultimately, the task or the job is prevented from being performed and thereby, the Government's objectivities are to that extent not attained. Different individuals react differently to the situation described above. A few resist firmly and pay the price; some offer passive resistance and try to do their best; what is worrisome is that an increasingly large number give in and reap the rewards of compliance. The major casualty is, of course, the total system.

While the conduct Rules provide for various opportunities to the officials in respect of proceedings of suspension, demotion, dismissal and minor penalties, they do not enjoy such safeguards as regards unjustified transfers. It is quite commonplace in several States to see mass transfers of senior officials at the district and secretarial level wherever there is a change of Government or leadership. It is often the case that the legitimate hierarchy for effecting the transfer and promotion of various officials is marginalised in favour of extra Constitutional systems based on extraneous influences. Consequently, not only is the ability and authority of the superior officials enforcing compliant action in the public interest by subordinate officials eroded, they become incapable of ensuring effective and responsive administration through lower level functionaries. At the same time, the system should provide for weeding out the non-performers on the basis of objective criteria.

The demand for stability of tenure and objective criteria for transfers and promotions is not only an element of motivation and efficient performance of civil servants, but is a matter of great concern for the public at large. It is seen that, when an official with sufficient knowledge of the district or city or the department is available a sufficiently long time to formulate policies, and implement schemes of poverty alleviation and the seven basic services in response to people's needs, effective governance is visible, especially in the context of the decentralisation of powers at the local level. This is seen from examples of excellent initiatives in this regard in districts or cities from officers with a long tenure and rapport with the citizens and their representatives, and the low level of development and utilisation of funds in districts or cities witnessing frequent rotation of officers. Further, the people can expect to receive fair, equitable treatment, unaffected by considerations of speed money benefits, only if the official is encouraged to have the courage and confidence to take decisions without fear or favour, or the penalty of premature transfer. These considerations are equally valid for the police and law enforcement agencies.

There has been a long-felt need for creation of an institutional arrangement for better personnel management at the State level. The Administrative Reform Commission in its report on State Administration in November 1969 had also felt the need for setting up an Establishment Board in each State for proper management of selction and posting for posts of the level of Under Secretary and above in the State Secretariats and field organisation. The matter has also been taken up in the Conference of Chief Secretaries held on the November 20, 1996. It had been concluded that the Government could be requested to devise suitable mechanisms, including punishment of a high powered civil services Board, and amend relevant rules for enabling transparent decisions on postings, promotions and transfers of senior officials on the lines of Central Government.

Such an institutional arrangement already exists in Government of India in the form of the Central Staffing Scheme. Under the Central Staffing Scheme of the Government of India, the Appointments Committee of the Cabinet (ACC) is empowered to take decision in respect of selection and appointments of officers to secretarial posts of and above the rank of Under Secretary to Government of India certain important non-secretarial posts as also on various other related issue of personnel management. In this respect, ACC is assisted and advised by the Civil services Board and the Central Establishment Board constituted therefor.

Though a complete transplant of the Central Staffing Scheme to the States is neither feasible nor desirable, it is suggested that the State Governments could consider intiating similar institutional arrangements. The true potential of the senior officials can be properly utilised for better management and development of the State. In this respect, guidelines for setting up the proposed Civil Services Board and its functions are enclosed herewith as Appendix.

These guidelines can become truly operative and generate credibility and morale in the civil services and the public only if Government employees are not permitted to bring political or other extraneous pressure to bear on the Government or on the transferring authorities for transfers and promotions. This issue is addressed in Code of Ethics. Any employee, who brings such pressures should be liable disciplinary action and in such cases strict punishment should be awarded. Such action should be initiated also in cases where references are received by Heads of Departments from outside agencies including political functionaries and members of the Public as well as bureaucrats for effecting transfers. It could be ensured that these guide are seen as carrying the authority of the Chief Minister so that a proper message goes down the entire system.

Proposed Action

The State Governments could consider adoption of the above mentioned scheme for setting up Civil Services Board with the proposed functions, for recommending the Chief Minister proposals on the transfer, promotion and placement of senior officials other than the Chief Secretary, DG of Police, and Chief Conservator of Forests, and for recommending action on grievances of officers, such as premature transfers or undue political pressure.

Appendix

Scheme for Civil Services Board

The proposed scheme will not apply to top functionaries like the Chief Secretary, Director General of Police and Chief Conservator of Forests who shall be apppointed by the Chief Minister as at present.

The State Government may set up a Civil Services Board, charged responsibility of recommending to the Government transfers and postings of all of and above the rank of Joint Secretary in the State Secretariat, apart from Heads of Departments, Additional Heads of Departments, Divisional Commissioners, Financial Commissioners, Collectors/District Magistrates and District Superintendents of police. The Board could comprise the following: (1) Chief Secretary-Chairman officer of the rank and status of Additional Chief Secretary (preferably the senior-most) or Chairman of the Board of Revenue or the senior-most Financial Commissioner, as the case may be in a State-Member: and (3) Secretary DOPT Secretary, Appointments, GAD, as the case may be in State-Member-Secretary.

The Home Secretary and DG of Police could be associated while considering matters relating to appointments at the level of DIG and above in the Home Department. The Secretary, Forest Department and the Principal CCF could be associated in connection with matters relating to the Conservator of Forests and above. Similarly, the Secretary of the Administrative Department concerned could be associated, as a special invitee, when a proposal concerning the Head of the Department Additional Head of that Department is being considered by the Board.

The Board's functions could be as under: (1) To recommend a panel o appointments to all posts mentioned in second paragraph above; (2) To All India Services officers and State service officers for their promotion short and long-term training within and outside the country; (3) To Government on personnel policy, especially career management of AIS officers and other State Civil Service officers; (4) To make proposals on transfers of such officers; and (5) To entertain appeals of officers against premature transfers and other grievances and submit the same with the Board's views to the Chief Minister.

The Board should meet on a pre-determined day of the week.

The merits of the suggested system would be: (1) Ensure more responsive and citizen-friendly administration, and effective execution of development schemes and programmes of poverty alleviation and welfare of weaker sections; (2) Appointments and promotions would be made after due consideration of all relevant factors and should be governed by the collective wisdom of the Board, while leaving the final decision to the political executive; (3) It would, over a period of time, make possible much greater accountability of officers in terms of performance and service to the people as, in the envisaged system, minimum tenures, say of two to five years or as per the norm prescribed by the Government; (4) Over time, with experience of the working of this system, more attention would begin to be paid to cadre management and career planning; and (5) The civil service and the public would benefit from the presence of officials who are impartial and committed to be values enshrined in the institution.

Any premature transfer before completion of prescribed tenure should be based on sound administrative grounds to be spelt out in the transfer order itself. Such premature transfer may be deemed to be a minor penalty, so that the officers have a right to appeal against such orders if they feel aggrieved, and summary procedures to deal with the situation.

In view of the importance of ensuring public confidence in the integrity and impartiality of the process of recruitment of candidates for public service, the selection of Chairman/Members of Public Service Commissions and Service Selection Boards should be done on the basis of recommendations of a similar committee.

Above all, there needs to be an agreement at the level of both the political executive and the top officials that the instrument of transfer should not be allowed to be misused by the civil servants or the politicians in power; nor should the power be vested in persons other than the constituted authorities of Government. As a matter of policy, pension of service should not be given to any employee.

With the increasing numbers of district development and municipal cadres, institutionalised and transparent systems of placement and career planning appear to be necessary to supplement this. The Government should continue the present practice of rotation in sensitive posts. Consideration for posting at the place of posting of the spouse, attention to the needs of women and the handicapped, etc.

Annexure XI

Supplementary Notes on Initiatives taken on Action Plan and Responsive Administration Government of India on Action Plan

The government of India has taken following initiatives on Action Plan:

1. Constitution of Working Group on Right to Information and Transparency to draft legislative proposals.
2. Steps to initiate formulation of Citizen's Charter by a number of Central Ministries and Departments with public interface, and introduction of

various citizen-friendly procedures and decentralised services by Railways, Posts, Telecom, Petroleum Ministry, Customs and Excise, Income Tax, etc.

3. Constitution of an Expert Group for Drawing up short-term and long-term plans for computerisation of Government operations and provision of services to the public, and steps already taken for computerisation in many Ministries.
4. Central scheme for computerisation for land records, digitisation of village cadastral maps, and consolidation of land holdings, with substantial benefits to cultivators, revenue administration, agricultural operations, etc.
5. Announcement of constitution of an independent Public Grievance Commission, as well as Police Complaints Authority for Delhi, speedy redressal of grievances relating to the Police on the one hand, and all the public utilities and departments of the Government of National Capital Territory of Delhi on the other. The Ministry of Home Affairs has set up a High-Level Committee with state representatives to examine various aspects relating to a more responsive administration citizen awareness of their rights modification to existing laws, etc., and to make recommendations in three months.
6. Operation of the Directorate of Public Grievances in the Cabinet Secretariat to entertain and decide finally on grievances relating to Central departments and agencies with a large public interface, such as telecommunications, passports, and insurance.
7. Introduction of a pilot scheme by the Department of Consumer Affairs and PDS to set up citizen information centres in selected cities, to be run by voluntary agencies, with links to the Public Services menu on the GISTNIC.
8. Support to national and state training institutions for training of officials at various levels in the emerging areas of economic reform, decentralisation, delivery of basic services, gender development, health care, primary education, AIDS control, nutrition, etc.
9. Operation of Staff Adalats in Railways, Posts and Telecom for continuous attention to the problems and grievances of the staff.
10. Operation of Lok Adalats in Telecom, Posts, etc., for satisfactory settlement of the problems of the people and consumers by face-to-face interaction and working of Social Audit panels, composed of eminent citizens, to listen to people's views and suggest improvements in the Posts and Telecom

11. Approval for the use of the Local Development Fund with M.P.'s for the installation of citizen Radio in Village Panchayats, public transport, etc., to provide emergency communication and two-way messages to the public.
12. Initiatives of the Ministry of Health and Family Welfare for upgradation of emergency facilities in major Central Government Hospitals in Delhi and system for regulation of private nursing homes through peer groups; the mobilisation of community participation and consumer awareness for safe food and drugs; and linkage of PHC's to extend secondary health services to the people in rural areas.
13. Formulation of a Code of Ethics for employees in public services.
14. Formulation of specific steps for steamlining the system of departmental enquiries and vigilance proceedings.
15. Steps for strict action against corruption and for integrity in public servants at all levels as, signified by the introduction of Lok Pal Bill in Parliament.
16. Constitution of an Efficiency Unit in the Cabinet Secretariat to undertake continuous exercise for delineation of Government functions, departmental re-structuring, procedural reforms, etc.

Initiatives on Responsive Administration

A number of initiatives have been taken by the State Governments and Central Government agencies in respect of responsive administration in recent years. These deserve to be studied and scaled up in the Central and State Governments as a whole, utilising wherever possible available funds in sectoral programmes. These need to be linked the decentralised delivery of services through elected local bodies on the following lines:

1. Improved sanitation and garbage collection with people's involvement in a number of cities like Surat, Pune and Chennai;
2. Taking 'grievance redressal to the people through mass contact and Lok Adalats at the village and neighbourhood levels;
3. Mass mobilisation schemes, such as Janmabhoomi and "Administration Going to the People' in Andhra Pradesh, bottom-up planning in Kerala, mass literacy campaigns etc.;
4. Computerisation land records and other information, and people-friendly revenue administration in a number of districts;
5. Giving one life-time certificate to the people as done in Andhra Pradesh by incorporating birth, nativity and caste certificates;
6. Setting up service counters for instant information and relief to the citizens in a number of Central Government Departments, like the Passport, Railways, Posts as well as the offices of Collectors;

7. Ensuring transparency and Right to Information to the people including making a provision for public hearings as done in States like Rajasthan and Madhya Pradesh, association of neighbourhood groups and citizen bodies in the planning and implementation of welfare schemes, planning and implementation of poverty alleviation and housing schemes, and empowerment of resident welfare groups as done in cities like Bangalore and Pune;
8. Establishing partnerships with voluntary agencies for health, nutrition and other schemes, and setting examples of inducting support from corporate sector;
9. Developing an innovative role of the AIR for grievance redressal as done in UP.

The Central and State Governments may take concerted measures for improved quality of administration and responsive services and schemes for the citizens through a package of multifaceted initiatives all of which will together help to promote accountable people-friendly government. These may include the following:

1. Wider accountability of all public servants for people-satisfaction and delivery of services according to a Citizens' Chartrer similar public statement of departmental goals.
2. Fullest possible decentralisation of service delivery, income support schemes and welfare activities through empowerment of elected rural and urban local bodies, accompanied by appropriate devolution of powers and resources in terms of the spirit and provisions of the 73rd and 74th Constitutional Amendments.
3. Encouragement to the widest possible awareness and participation of citizens and representative groups and voluntary agencies in the formation and implementation of schemes as already envisaged in ongoing sectoral schemes and in the Five Years Plan document.
4. Simplification and clarity in forms and procedures, with arrangements for setting up citizen information centres in all the districts and towns.
5. Transparent procedures and criteria for beneficial identification in the provision of services and subsidies, the operation of the public distribution system, etc., to ensure that the benefits fully reach the poor and the disadvantaged, alongwith a system of public hearings to facilitate consultation by the public at the local level.
6. Giving the citizens widespread and easy access to all information relating to Government operations and laws, and reversing the undue emphasis on secrecy surrounding award of tenders and procurement, identification of beneficiaries, allotment of various assets, admission to colleges and schools, recruitment for jobs, etc.

7. Steps to enact legislation for Freedom of Information, amendments to the Official Secrets Act, Codes of Conduct, rules for classification of records, etc.
8. Training and orientation of both officials and elected representatves at all levels, steps to upgrade their skills, access to technological and computerised aids for information processing and storage, top-level support by delegation of powers and workplace improvement and rewards for good performance.
9. Equipping and orienting all public offices and delivery centres to provide quick and responsive delivery of public services, grievance redressal and information to the public, alongwith convergent services for target groups in areas of basic services identified by the Conference of Chief Ministers in July, 1996.

Select Bibliography

Administrative Reforms Commission. Report on Centre-state Relationships. New Delhi: Manager, Publication Branch, 1969.

Administrative Staff College. Accountability of government departments. London: ASC, 1955.

Ahluwalia, Isher Judge, Rakesh Mohan and Omkar Goswami, Policy reform in India. New Delhi: Oxford and IBH, 1996.

Alatas, Syed Hussein. Corruption: its nature, causes and functions. Aldershot: Avebury, 1990.

All India Management Association, Corporate governance and business ethics. New Delhi: Excel Books, 1997.

Anand, D.A. Electoral reforms : curbing role of money power. New Delhi: Indian Institute of Public Administration, 1995.

Andhyarujina, T.R. Judicial activism and constitutional democracy in India. Bombay : N.M. Tripathi, 1992.

Arora, Ramesh K. Peopl's participation in development process. Jaipur : HCM RIPA, 1979.

Banerjee, Ajit M. and K. A. Chandrasekaran. Renewing governance: issues and options. New Delhi: McGraw-Hill, 1996.

Banerjee, S.K. Forty years after independence: The change in India. New Delhi: Enkay, 1994.

Barker, James Jr., Bernard Tenenbaum and Fiona Woolf. Governance and regulation of power pools and system operators: an international comparison. Washington, D.C. The World Bank, 1997.

Barve, S.G., Good government : The administrative malaise and connected issues. New Delhi: Indian Institute of Public Administration, 1964.

Baxi, Upendra. Annual capital foundation lecture 1996: on judicial activism, legal education and research in a globalising India. New Delhi : Capital Foundation Society, 1996.

Betes, Robert H. and Anne O. Krueger, eds. Political and economic interactions in economic policy reform. Oxford: Blackwell, 1993.

Bhambri, C.P. Bureaucracy and politics in India. Delhi : Vikas, 1971.

Bhargava, G.S. India's Watergate: study of political corruption in India. Delhi : Arnold Publishers, 1974.

Bhargava, G.S. Indira's India gate : latest study of political corruption in India. Delhi : Arnold-Heinemann Publishers, 1974.

Bhattacharya, Mohit. Restructuring public administration: essays in rehabilitation. New Delhi : Jawahar, 1997.

Bhushan, Prashant. Bofors: the selling of a nation. New Delhi: Vision, 1990.

Birkenshaw, When citizen's complain: reforming justice and administration. Buckingham: Open University Press, 1993.

Bueno Mesquita, Bruce. Strategy, risk and personality in coalition politics: the case of India. Cambridge: Cambridge University Press, 1975.

Caiden, Gerald E., ed. Strategies for administrative reform. Lexington Mass D.C. Health, 1982.

Chapman, Richard A. and JR. Greenway. The dynamics of administrative reform. London: Croom Helm, 1980.

Chatterjee, Partha, ed. State and politics in India. Delhi: Oxford Univ. Press, 1997.

Chaturvedi, T.N., ed. Perspectives of administrative reforms for integrated rural development: India. New Delhi: Indian Institute of Public Administration, 1980.

Chaturvedi, T.N., ed. Quest for commitment in public services. New Delhi: Department of Personnel and Administrative Reforms, 1975.

Chaturvedi, T.N., ed. Secrecy in government. New Delhi: Indian Institute of Public Administration, 1980.

Chaturvedi, T.N. and S. Venugopal Rao, eds. Police administration. New Delhi: Indian Institute of Public Administration, 1982.

Chaturvedi, T.N. ed. Ethics in public life. New Delhi: Indian Institute of Public Administration, 1996.

Chaturvedi, T.N., ed. Contemporary administrative culture of India. New Delhi: Indian Institute of Public Administration, 1996.

Chaturvedi, T.N., ed. Administrative accountability. New Delhi: Indian Institute of Public Administration, 1984.

Chitkara, M.G. Corruption N cure. Delhi: APH Publication, 1997.

Chopra, S.K., ed. Towards good governance. Delhi: Konark, 1997.

Consumer Coordination Council. An insight into Citizen's Charter. New Delhi: CCC, December 1997.

Coolidge, Jacqueline and Susan Rose-Ackerman. High-level rent-seeking and corruption in African regimes: theory and cases. Washington, D.C.: The World Bank, 1997.

Dwivedi, Onkar P., R.B. Jain and Dhirendra K. Vajpeyi, eds. Governing India: issues concerning public policy, institutions and administration. Delhi: BR. Publishing, 1998.

Dwivedy, Surendranath and G.S. Bhargava. Political corruption in India. Delhi: Popular, 1967.

Echeverri-Gent, John. The State and the poor: public policy and political development in India and the United States. Oxford: Univ. of California Press, 1993.

Faundez, Julio, ed. Good government and law: legal and institutional reform in developing countries. London: Macmillan, 1997.

Frischtak, Leila L. Governance capacity and economic reform in Developing Countries. Washington, D.C.: The World Bank, 1994.

Gadkari, S.S. Electoral reforms in India. New Delhi: Wheeler Pub., 1996.

Geist, B. State audit: developments in public accountability. London: Macmillan, 1981.

Gill, S.S. The pathology of corruption. New Delhi: Harper Collins, 1998.

Girling, John. Corruption, capitalism and democracy. London: Routledge, 1997.

Gopalsawami, R.A. Indian polity: a plea for reform. Bombay: Nachiketa, 1970.

Gruber, Judith E. Controlling bureaucracies: dilemmas in democratic governance. Berkeley: University of California Press, 1987.

Guhan, S. and Samuel Paul, eds. Corruption in India: agenda for action. New Delhi: Vision Books, 1997.

Gupta, Deepak. Corporate social accountability: disclosures and practices. New Delhi: Mittal Pub., 1995.

Gupta, M.C. and R.K. Tiwari, eds. Restructuring government. New Delhi: Indian Institute of Public Administration, 1998.

Haggard, Stephan and Steven B. Webb, eds. Voting for reform: democracy, political liberalization, and economic adjustment. Washington, D.C.: The World Bank, 1994.

Heidenheimer, Arnold J. Political corruption: readings in comparative analysis. New York: Holt, 1970.

Held, David. Democracy and the global order: from the modern state to cosmopolitan governance. Cambridge: Polity Press, 1995.

Heywood, Paul, ed. Political corruption. Oxford: Blackwell, 1997.

Hoen, Herman W., Editor, Good Governance in Central and Eastern Europe: The puzzle of Capitalism by Design, Northampton, MA: Edward Elga, 2001.

India. Administrative Reforms Commission. Study Team. Reports. New Delhi: The Commission, India. Cabinet Secretariat. Department of Personnel and Administrative Reforms. New perspectives for public administration in India. New Delhi : Training Division, 1975.

India. Committee on Electoral Reforms. Report of the Committee on Electoral Reforms. New Delhi: Legislative Department, Ministry of Law and Justice, 1990.

India. Committee on Prevention of Corruption. Report. Delhi: Controller of Publications, 1964 (Chairman K. Santhanam).

Indian Institute of Public Administration, New Delhi. Conference on administrative reforms: Proceedings. New Delhi: IIPA, 1967.

Indian Institute of Public Administration, New Delhi. Electoral reforms. New Delhi: IIPA, 1994.

International Monetary Fund, Washington D.C., Good Governance: The IMF's Role, 1997.

Jabbra, Joseph G. and O.P. Dwivedi, eds. Public service accountability: a comparative perspective. West Hartford: Kumarian Press, 1988.

Kashyap, Subhash C., ed. Crime and corruption to good governance. New Delhi: Uppal, 1997.

Kashyap, Subhash C., ed. Judicial activism and Lokpal. New Delhi: Uppal, 1997.

Kaushik, Asha. Democratic concerns: the Indian experience. Jaipur: Alekh, 1994.

Klitgaard, Robert. Controlling corruption. Berkeley: Univ. of California Press, 1988.

Koehler, Jerry W. and Joseph M. Pankowski. Quality government: designing, developing and implementing TQM. Florida: St Lucie Press, 1996.

Kohli, Atul. Democracy and discontent India's growing crisis of Government. Cambridge: Cambridge University Press, 1991.

Kothari, Shanti and Ramashray Roy. Relations between politicians and administrators at the district level: a study for the Administrative reforms Commission. Government of India. Delhi: Indian Institute of Public Administration, 1981.

Kousar J. Azam, ed. Federalism and good governance: issues across cultures. New Delhi: South Asian, 1998.

Nepali, Rohitakumara, Good Governance: A Dream or Reality? Kathmandu: SAP-N Publishing House, 2000.

Nye, Joseph S. and John D. Dohahue, eds., Governance in a Globalizing World, Cambridge, MA.: Vision of Governance for the 21st Century, Washington, DC., Brookings Institution, 2000.

Page, W., ed. The future of politics: governance, movements and world order. London: Frances Pinter, 1983.

Paranjpe, Nalini. Administrative reforms in India. New Delhi: Uppal, 1997.

Paul, Samuel. Accountability in public services: exit, voice and capture. Washington, D.C.: The World Bank, 1991.

Paul, Samuel. Strengthening public service accountability: a conceptual framework. Washington, D.C.: IBRD, 1991.

Pavarale, Vinod. Interpreting corruption: elite perspective in India. New Delhi: Sage, 1996.

Prasad, A.D. Corruption and administration. Patna: Basant Pub., 1971.

Rao, G.R.S., ed. Accountability of public institutions: emerging issues in the Indian context. Hyderabad: Rajaji International Institute of Public Affairs and Administration, 1991.

Rhodes, Raw. Understanding governance: policy networks. Open University Press, 1997.

Rose, Richard, ed. Challenge to governance: studies in overloaded polities. Beverly Hills: Sage, 1980.

Rose-Ackerman, Susan. Corruption: a study in political economy. New York: Academic Press, 1978.

Sen Gupta, Bhabani. India: problems of governance. Delhi: Konark, 1996.

Sharma, Raju. Foundations of the principle of transparency in government. New Delhi: Indian Institute of Public Administration, 1998.

Singh, Naunihal. A system of governance: parliamentary or presidential. New Delhi: Anmol, 1998.

Sinha, Ajit Kumar, ed. New economic policy of India: restructuring and liberalising the economy for 21st Century. New Delhi: Deep and Deep, 1994.

Sinha, V.M. The superior civil services in India: a study in administrative development: 1947-57. Jaipur: The Institute for Research and Advanced Studies, 1985.

Smith-Sreen, Poonam. Accountability in development organization: experiences of women's organizations in India. New Delhi: Sage, 1995.

UK Efficiency Unit. Making things happen: a report on the implementation of government efficiency scrutinies, by Kate Jenkins, Graham Oates and Andrew Stott. London: HMSO, 1985.

Ward, Peter M., ed. Corruption, development and inequality: soft touch or hard graft. London: Routledge, 1989.

Williamson, Oliver E. The mechanisms of governance. New York: Oxford Univ. Press, 1996.

Willimson, John, ed. The political economy of policy reform.

Woodiwiss, Michael. Crime, crusades and corruption: prohibitions in the United States, 1900-1987. London: Pinter, 1988.

Yates, Douglas. Bureaucratic democracy: the search for democracy and efficiency in American Government. Cambridge, Mass.: Harvard Univ. Press, 1982.

Young, Oran R. Global governance: drawing insights from the environmental experience. Cambridge: MIT Press, 1997.

Articles

Agarwal, U C, Rising Corruption, Low Convictions South Asia Politics Vol. 1, 4th August, 2002, pp. 13-14.

Behera, Manas, Globalization and Governance in India, South Asia Politics Vol. 3, 3rd July, 2004, pp. 35-37.

Bhatt, Yusuf, Good Governance, A promise for justice, Indian Journal of Political Science, Vol. LXV No. 2 April-June 2004, pp. 221-235.

Biju, M R, Panchayati Raj in India under threats, South Asia Politics Vol. 1, March 2003, pp. 47-50.

Bopanna, P P, ICS, IAS and Adminstrative Law in India, South Asia Politics Vol. 1, 9th January 2003, pp. 39-44.

Bopanna, P P, Adminstration of Criminal Justice in India after Independence, South Asia Politics Vol. 2, 1st May 2003, pp. 31-35.

Chopra B, Myth of Financial Accountability, Politics India, Vol. 1 No. 7, pp. 43-44.

Dubhashi, P R, Reforms with Human Face, South Asia Politics Vol. 3, 8th December, 2004, pp. 36-38.

Dutta, Ranjan, Governance and Development in Assam, South Asia Politics Vol. 2, 6th October 2003, pp. 41-47.

Gehlot, N S, Meaning of Good Governance and its Relevance in the functioning of Indian Democracy, South Asia Politics, Vol. 3, No. 2, June 2004, pp. 14-18.

Gupta, K L, Ethics in Public Administration, South Asia Politics Vol. 1, 9th January 2003, pp. 36-38.

Halan, Y C, Why India is Successful Democracy but failed Polity? South Asia Politics Vol. 3, 8th December, 2004.

Jain, R B, Innovations and Reforms in Indian Administration in V. Grover (Ed.) Political System and Constitution of India, Deep & Deep Publication, New Delhi, 1997.

Jha, Nalini Kant, Need for Judicial Accountability, South Asia Politics Vol. 1, 9th January 2003, pp. 33-35.

Kulkarni, Manu N, Competitive Politics for Good Governance, Deccan Herald, Friday, April 23, 2004.

Murtaza, Naheed, Dimensions and Dynamics of Corrupt Practice in Indian Polity and an Operational Paradigm of Judicial, Ethical and Political Measures, Indian Journal of Politics, Vol. XXXVII, No. 4, Oct.-Dec. 2003, pp. 28-32.

Muthamma, C B, Towards Just Society, South Asia Politics Vol. 1, 8th December, 2002, pp. 26-28.

Muthamma, C B, A Tainted System, South Asia Politics Vol. 3, 7th November, 2004, pp. 22-26.

Parthasarthy, R., Misgovernance: India's Bame, The Hindu, Tuesday 10th September, 2002.

Rao, G R S, Regression of Constitutional Democracy, South Asia Politics Vol. 3, 8th December, 2004, pp. 29-32.

Roy, Ramashray, State Against Society, South Asia Politics Vol. 3, May 2004, pp. 8-16.

Shahabuddin, Syed, District Reorganization in UP, South Asia Politics Vol. 3, 1st May 2004, pp. 32-36.

Singh, Ravindra Pal, Good Governance for Security Sector Reforms, South Asia Politics Vol. 1, 12th April 2003, pp. 38-46.

Sinha, Shivendra K, Implementing Agenda for Good Governance, South Asia Politics Vol. 1, 4th August, 2002, pp. 18-22.

Trivedi, Prabhat Kumar, Politics, Politicians and Good Governance, South Asia Politics Vol.1-2, 11th March, 2004, pp. 39-41.

Tyagi, Ruchi, Electoral Reforms: From Seshan to Krishnamurthy, South Asia Politics Vol. 3, 3rd July, 2004, pp. 27-34.

Venkataramana, M (Et. Al.), Woman Participation in Decentralised Local Self Governance, South Asia Politics Vol. 3, 4th August, 2004, pp. 26-33.